IT'S EASY BEING GREEN

IT'S EASY BEING GREEN
A Handbook for Earth-Friendly Living

Crissy Trask

Illustrations by Mike Clelland

Gibbs Smith, Publisher
Salt Lake City

First Edition
10 09 08 07   9 8

Text © 2006 Crissy Trask
Illustrations © 2006 Mike Clelland

Published by
Gibbs Smith, Publisher
P.O. Box 667
Layton, Utah 84041

Orders: 1.800.748.5439
www.gibbs-smith.com

Designed by Martin Yeeles
Printed and bound in Canada

Library of Congress Cataloging-in-Publication Data

Trask, Crissy.
  It's easy being green : a handbook for earth-friendly living / Crissy
Trask ; illustrations by Mike Clelland.— 1st ed.
      p. cm.
  Includes bibliographical references.
    ISBN 10: 1-58685-772-X   ISBN 13: 978-1-58685-772-1
1. Environmental protection—Citizen participation.
2. Environmentalism. 3. Organic living. I. Title.

TD171.7.T73 2006
333.72—dc22

2005027473

For my husband.

CONTENTS

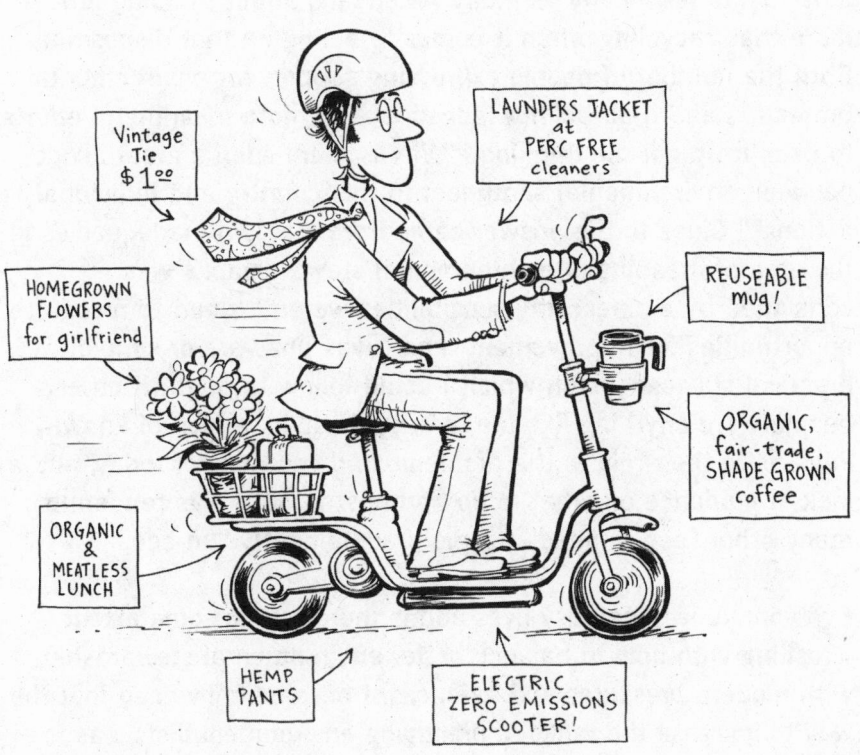

INTRODUCTION

Many Americans agree with the goals of the environmental movement. Yet, nearly as many Americans admit to doing little more than recycling when it comes to acting on that disposition. Both the number of people expressing support for environmental protection and their acknowledged lack of more meaningful efforts to back it up got me thinking, "Why is there such a great divide between environmental sentiment in this country and individual actions?" Clues to the answer came from my own inadequacies in the area of meaningful environmental stewardship. I was consumed by a career, my sensibilities weren't tuned to recognize opportunities for improvement, and I was unaware of simple, practical suggestions on which I could follow through. If other people were anything like me, a busy lifestyle, a lack of knowledge as to their role in the problems and solutions of today, and a lack of guidance on what to do and how to do it was rendering many other "eco-minded" people predominantly "un-eco."

Everyone is leading busy lives and is therefore, to some extent, wrestling with how to balance better environmental stewardship with modern pressures and reliances. I became convinced that the way to increase the ranks of *practicing* environmentalists was to take the difficulty and guesswork out of greener living—by adjusting expectations, stressing learning as a motivator and enabler, and above all else, providing constructive tips and resources to prepare the eco-inclined for action on terms they could live with. It made sense that if busy people were going to start doing more, they would need a lot more help.

It's Easy Being Green is a remedy for that which has held back more people from making better choices for the environment: inadequate information, the uncertainty of what to do, the apprehension of activism and lagging motivation. This is a book that supplies what the busy person needs to start making changes today. It cultivates an appreciation for the cause-and-effect relationship between actions and real environmental harm; it prescribes practical and actionable solutions that can be carried out without aggravation; it promotes the gradual integration of new behaviors and solutions in order to retain what is learned and sustain improvements; and it includes Internet resources and tools for the distinct help they can provide with great ease and efficiency.

This book provides the conscientious reader with a new or renewed consciousness to recognize the need and occasions for improvements and concurrently presents a plan, tips and resources that busy people can use to follow through on good intentions. If you haven't invested in substantially greener behaviors, consumerism and politics because you didn't know how or thought it was difficult, help is here: *It's Easy Being Green* is a handbook for all those who aspire do more to protect the environment but want it to be simpler.

CHAPTER 1:
GREEN LIVING MYTHS

Present-day trends include disappearing wilderness and farmland, irresponsible consumerism, the poisoning of our waterways, species decline and an arguably corrupt political system that panders to exploitative special interests. Turning the tide on such destructive and discouraging trends requires all of us to learn to appreciate how our own behaviors contribute to these problems and to recognize opportunities and occasions to act in ways that can reverse these trends or at least diminish their impacts.

Adopting better habits and ways of doing things doesn't require riches, inordinate discretionary time or overhauling your life, but these could be a few of the misperceptions that inhibit more Americans from acting on their predilection for a healthy environment. Disabusing some common myths about greener living may help remove remaining apprehensions about committing to and acting on some meaningful changes that will enrich your life and make a difference to our world. Consider the following myths and the truths behind them.

"The problems that exist in the world today cannot be solved by the level of thinking that created them." **Albert Einstein**

EARTH-FRIENDLY LIVING IS A VIRTUE, NOT AN OBLIGATION.

It is now common knowledge that the biggest problems facing our global environment stem from human activities. If these problems are to be arrested or remedied, who else but humans will turn the tide? It's not virtue that produces results when taking on many of life's challenges head on. It's only with a sense of purpose and responsibility that great things are achieved. Be it career, family or the environment, as a society, and personally, we are obligated to put forth a certain amount of effort to succeed in achieving what we need to live and protecting what has value. Our obligation to at least try to pay our own way in life, raise our children into healthy, productive and ethical members of society, and lighten our impact on the earth, among other things, is real.

IT WILL BE TOO DIFFICULT AND DISRUPTIVE TO CHANGE MY HABITS.

There may be a period of adjustment as you embark on turning bad habits into better ones, but difficult and disruptive hardly describe the changes prescribed in this book. Especially when you consider that changing habits and situations can occur a little at a time and over the course of many weeks, making corrections manageable. Changes do not have to be immediately broad and uncompromising. You can start by making small and simple improvements and build on them.

After doing something a certain way long enough, it becomes automatic, but just because something has become automatic doesn't mean that replacing it will be difficult. Forming new eco-friendly behaviors is simply a process of time, repetition and growth. Even in areas where you may have deep-rooted habits, rethinking the full experience and implications of those habits can reveal how unsuitable they really are. Take our dependence on the automobile, for example: do we love asphalt landscapes, traffic jams, road rage, brown skylines and filling our tanks at the pump? Much of the driving people do is more of a habit than a convenience, pleasure or necessity. And like all habits we want to break, we need only find a new one to replace it. Reducing how many days we do the driving—and letting a carpool buddy or public transit worker pick up the slack—reduces stress, accidents and traffic as well as expenses for gas, insurance, tickets, parking and vehicle maintenance. Giving up your car two to three days a week when transportation alternatives exist isn't a hardship, it's just an adjustment.

EARTH-FRIENDLY PRODUCTS ARE HARD TO FIND AND EXPENSIVE.

The natural and sustainable products industry is estimated to be a $230 billion industry nationally, growing by 20 to 30 percent annually. There are thought to be approximately 13,000 retailers devoted to selling environmentally preferable products,[1] and conventional retailers, not wanting to lose traditional customers who are "going green," have begun integrating safer, natural and sustainable alternatives into their assortment. (The easiest way to find out what conventional retailers are offering in the way of lower-impact products is to go to their Web site and search for keywords like "recycled" or "organic." Any and all products with descriptions containing your keywords will be revealed to you.) And there are countless more green businesses operating exclusively on the Web. Finding green products is easier than ever and getting easier all the time.

As far as price, many earth-friendly products are as economical, or more so, as their conventional counterparts because they often utilize recycled or reclaimed materials, require less processing and output less waste than would otherwise have to be managed. There are also many examples of deferred savings after an initially higher expenditure—as in the case of energy-efficient products that reduce energy costs in the long run.

Some earth-friendly alternatives do cost a bit more than their conventional equivalent at the present time, but a well-rounded green buying strategy that includes seeking out energy-efficient, enduring and used products—all of which save you money—can bring down your total average expenditures.

IF I TURN MY BACK ON CONVENTIONAL BUSINESSES, THE ECONOMY WILL SUFFER.

In the expanded marketplace of wisdom and emerging alternatives, "conventional" applies to companies, practices and products that persist in a standard or traditional use of disfavored practices and materials when environmentally preferable ones are both technologically and financially viable. Now that we're clear on the definition of "conventional," let's explore the fallacies in the belief that deviating from the status quo in purchasing will cause the nation's economy great harm.

A shift in consumer loyalties is typical in a market economy. It is a fundamental precept for a strong market economy and a catalyst for economic prosperity. Demand for new and different products and technologies gives rise to new markets—spawning innovation, competition, investment, market growth and jobs. For example, rejecting fuel-inefficient vehicles, the majority of a typical automaker's product assortment, in favor of an electric/gasoline hybrid car will only result in the decline of traditional automakers if they choose to ignore the emerging trend. Corporations are in business to stay in business, and under good leadership, they will change with consumer demand to stay relevant and competitive. Those companies that won't change will quickly be replaced by businesses that can meet consumer demand—sustaining a robust and viable economy.

Furthermore, it's absolutely necessary that our consumer choices support less wasteful and harmful products and cleaner, sustainable production of the things we need. Economies are only as sustainable as the ecosystems and resources they rely upon year after year. As the head of the United Nations Environment Programme said, "Ecosystems and the services they provide are financially significant and . . . to degrade and damage them is tantamount to economic suicide." Companies that don't respect this certainty, but have your business anyway, will have no incentive to make modifications. Therefore, turning your back on conventional businesses that you have judged to be unaccountable for their actions and disrespecting to the earth is the most important thing you can do to protect our economic future. There is more on this subject in the next chapter.

"The man who goes alone can start today; but he who travels with another must wait till that other is ready." **Henry David Thoreau**

PEOPLE DISPLAYING "GREEN LIVING" PREFERENCES AND BEHAVIORS CAN LOOK CHEAP AND ECCENTRIC.

To some yes, but only to those that are out of touch with emerging trends and the needs of our society and environment. The manifestations of acute intelligence and enlightenment have always been perceived as a bit eccentric—right? In all seriousness, though, most people know enough to accurately judge displays of thrift and conservation for what they are—and respect them—even if this isn't expressed. Those closest to you will certainly know the origin of, and goodness of, for example, your insistence on reusing items several times that most would discard after one use or your efforts to save grey water for use in the garden. As for anyone who doesn't know you, and doesn't get it, their opinion of you shouldn't matter.

THE FRUGALITY THAT GREENER LIVING REQUIRES MEANS DEPRIVING ME AND MY FAMILY OF COMFORTS OF LIFE AND CONVENIENCES I'VE EARNED.

Reasonable comforts and conveniences needn't be sacrificed when committing to greener living. A scale or quantity you're accustomed to may need to be reduced, but the ingenuity and innovation inherent within a capitalist system like ours, often the target of disdain by environmentalists, has nonetheless produced many products enabling earth-minded people to live the good life if this is important to them. Designer home furnishings, state-of-the-art appliances, a nice car, fine cuisine, exotic vacations—these can all be found in earth-friendly form. Just because you're not currently familiar with resources that can provide all these things and more, doesn't mean they don't exist.

Whatever your pet comforts and conveniences are, there is most likely a substitute that will prove to be equally or more satisfying when all the facts are in. Adopting a greener lifestyle doesn't have to be an exercise in deprivation unless that is your choice. Greener living can be compatible with modern living through a process of reconciliation, discovery and integration: reconciliation of your ideals, discovery of replacements and integration of those replacements into your life. You'll soon realize that what you're losing is an advantage and a relief, and what you're gaining is infinitely more satisfying: a healthier, simpler, more balanced life that will have the Joneses envying you.

SUPPORTING ENVIRONMENTAL CAUSES MEANS GIVING UP TIME I DON'T HAVE (E.G., VOLUNTEERING AND WRITING LOTS OF LETTERS).

Today's busy student, professional or caregiver doesn't need to lead campaigns and construct manifestos to have their opinions counted. The Internet has made it easier than ever to acquire timely information on actionable issues and send pre-written letters of support or protest that target decision makers.

Organizations working on a range of issues from environmental protection to corporate and government accountability are enabling people to take action from the privacy of their home or office with very little time spent. Anyone with access to a computer and the Internet can sign petitions and send letters to decision makers just by going online. It's never been simpler to participate in influencing environmental policy. *Chapter 6: Getting Involved* discusses this subject at some length.

IT'S HYPOCRITICAL TO ADVOCATE AND PRACTICE ENVIRONMENTALLY FRIENDLY BEHAVIORS IN SOME, BUT NOT ALL, AREAS OF MY LIFE.

Greener living is a relative and evolving state. Being somewhere between the beginning and the middle (there really is no "end") of a journey entailing discovery, evaluation and adaptation automatically means that there will always be questions, more to do and things you could do better.

Hypocrisy comes into play only if you give false information about your attributes or demand a standard from another that you won't live up to yourself. If you scold your neighbor for wasting water in their yard, you best be practicing water conservation on your side of the fence. But possessing the desire and intention to live greener, while having made only marginal progress to date, doesn't make you a hypocrite, it makes you imperfect. And aren't we all?

Be patient with yourself and your critics who would prefer you abandon your goals to make themselves feel better. Learning to live greener is a process that takes time, and you shouldn't have unrealistic expectations that could sabotage your drive and eventual success. What you're able to achieve is a factor of understanding, timing, location, obligations, finances, and so many other things, so adopt a willingness to be a work in progress—it's really the only way to learn and improve.

NOTHING I DO WILL MAKE A DIFFERENCE IF NO ONE ELSE IS DOING ANYTHING.

No one is alone in their concern for the environment and their conscience to act more thoughtfully to protect its well-being. Your efforts to walk lighter on this earth, support green capitalism and appeal for better environmental policy make a difference, because every act, when multiplied over many days and many people, produces positive results. Remember, even if those changes can't be seen, they are still occurring.

So many people making efforts, large and small, to green their lives adds up to big results for the environmental movement, not only for the cumulative impact of numerous individual actions, but also for the power that one person's example has to bring about positive changes in others. Every day people all over the world exhibit ecological behaviors that raise consciousness and elicit duplication from others who witness them. Change yourself and you will unwittingly change another.

CHAPTER 2:
MAKING A DIFFERENCE

Within the domains of daily living, purchasing and taking action lie our opportunities and our obligations to effect positive change in the world. Every day in this country more than 290 million people go about their lives—lives that in some way impact the natural environment for better or worse. Understanding the relationship between what we do and the larger environment is vital to developing and strengthening a sense of responsibility for the cause and effect of our actions. With new knowledge and a new appreciation for our role in the solution, we can begin to implement meaningful changes.

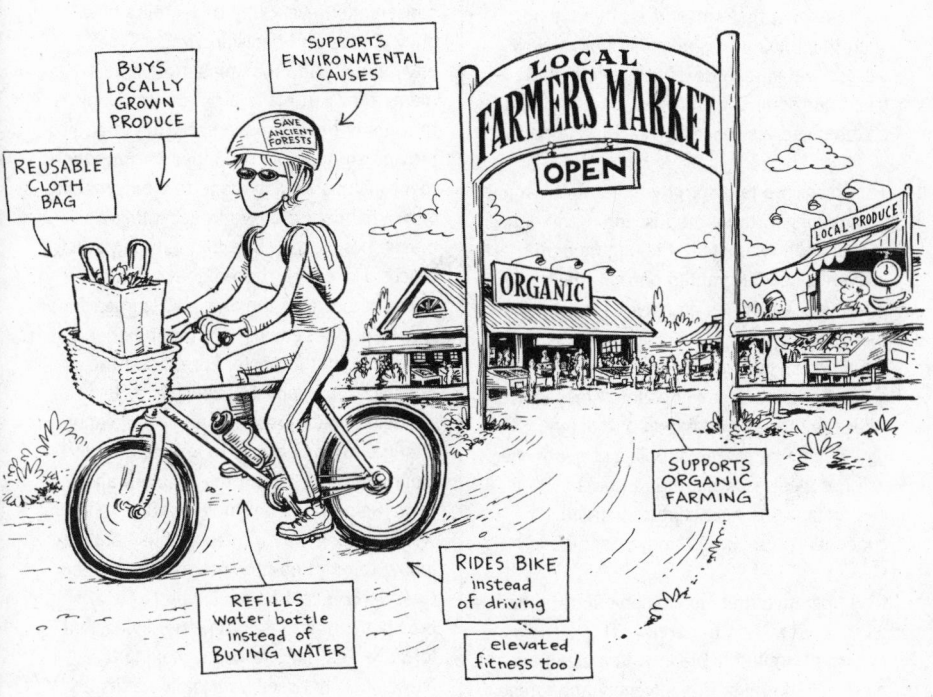

DAILY LIVING

Daily living encompasses the choices we make for ourselves and our family every day, the actions that follow our choices and the consequences of it all. In a crowded world of disappearing, finite resources, there is no such thing as an insignificant choice. How we use water, dispose of used products, clean our homes, get around, and feed and clothe ourselves, have far-reaching impacts.

The things we take for granted simply cannot be any longer; there are just too many of us. In this country, contently taking modern conveniences for granted doesn't make us privileged—it makes us naïve. The water that runs from our tap, for example, is not the limitless resource we may think it is; it is a finite and increasingly polluted resource. With the human population outpacing renewable freshwater, supplies of freshwater will not meet ecosystem and human demands in the next century without concerted preservation and conservation.[1]

It's imperative that we conserve and protect all that we rely on to survive. This includes but is not limited to clean water, clean air, productive farmland, biodiversity and forest-land—and it's all related. We cannot protect our water supply without also protecting our wetlands and forests. We cannot sustain biodiversity without protecting habitat for wildlife and preserving productive farmland. When one thing suffers, so does the rest— you can count on it.

TURNING THINGS AROUND

People can turn things around by making small, incremental efforts to green their lives today—and then keep going. You can accomplish meaningful preservation and conservation every day by learning how daily chores and decisions impact the environment and making simple adjust-ments that can make a difference. Choices that many people make every day that also provide suitable opportunities for improve-ment include driving alone to work, making one-sided copies at work, accepting a plastic bag at the store and ignoring a leaky faucet. For some, these behaviors may continue because they haven't learned to associate the behavior with its broader environmental impacts. For others, the behavior may persist because they lack acquaintance with solutions or motivation to change. In any case, a more acute under-standing of our role in the problem and some helpful tips on implementing solutions will go a long way in helping busy people follow through on changes for the better. *Chapter 3: Eco-Tips for Living Greener* provides ample tips for greener living, but for now, you need to begin making the association between your daily habits and the environment at large. The following examples illustrate how popular, everyday actions impact the environment, and likewise, how simple corrections can make a real difference.

> "Nobody made a greater mistake than he who did nothing because he could do only a little." **Edmund Burke**

Bag It, Please

How did checkout at the local grocer end up being an exercise in so much needless environmental harm and resource waste? In a word, "plastic." The evolution of plastic bags into the preferred choice for most supermarket shoppers is a great curiosity: they accommodate relatively few items; pile up at home faster than new second uses can be invented for them; and have a tendency to blow away, making them a prevalent source of litter. These reasons alone would prompt most people to try something else—and about 20 percent of shoppers do ask for paper,[2] but paper and plastic both have environmental impacts that provide compelling reasons to abstain from using either.

Plastic bags are made from nonrenewable petroleum resources and require the use of toxic chemicals during production and processing. Plastics production produces 14 percent of toxic air emissions in the United States, and each plant emits an average of 300 to 500 gallons of contaminated wastewater per minute.[3] As plastic bags move through their life cycle, they continue to menace the environment. Very few facilities collect and recycle plastic bags, and they end up primarily as litter or landfill material. In Rhode Island alone, more than 870 tons of plastic bags are thrown away per year—or 95 percent of all plastic bags used in the state.[4] Loose in the environment by the billions due to their propensity to blow away, plastic bags are not only unsightly, they can harm or kill wildlife. Those that do make it to a landfill will last for several lifetimes.

Paper has its problems too: every year nearly 900 million trees are cut down to provide raw materials for American paper and pulp mills.[5] Contributing to this figure are the 10 billion brown paper grocery bags used annually in supermarkets across the country[6] requiring virgin fibers to give them the strength to hold up to heavy groceries. Pulp and paper mills are also among the worst polluters of air, water and land of any manufacturing industry in the country.

Plastic and paper bags are not only less desirable from an environmental standpoint; they are also functionally inferior to stronger reusable carriers, and thus quite impractical. The smart and resource-wise choice is to use durable cloth carriers—preferably ones made from organically grown fibers—for everyday shopping. Significant environmental harm and a portion of our waste stream would disappear if everyone started using cloth bags in place of paper or plastic. This is an easy and immensely practical daily choice, and the hardest part is remembering to take cloth bags with you to the store. Practice helps, and so does leaving a set with your vehicle at all times.

Do I Hear Water Running?

Less than 1 percent of the water supply on earth is available for human consumption, and our long-term supply of clean water is being threatened by depletion and pollution. Each day we are confronted with many decisions that affect water. We make a water decision every time we turn on the tap, choose to overlook a leak or pour grey water down the drain.

In one day, the average person uses up to 183 gallons of water for drinking, cooking, washing, flushing and watering,[7] yet it is estimated that normal and efficient household use could save 31 percent of that, or 57 gallons a day per person.[8] Given this appraisal of residential misuse, the occasions for conserving water are abundant. Even more encouraging is the simplicity of conservation.

Opportunities for conservation can be either economic or behavioral. An economic modification would include installing water-efficient fixtures and systems. Most fixture modifications are simple, inexpensive and immediately effective. Installing a low-flow showerhead can save a family of four 20,000 gallons of water a year and costs just $5. Faucet aerators, which reduce the water use at a faucet by as much as 60 percent while still maintaining a strong flow, are an inexpensive way to save up to three gallons of water a minute during use. In the yard, a drip irrigation system installed around outdoor plants prevents evaporation and waste from inefficient watering. And adding timers to outdoor spigots to regulate sprinklers can save incalculable amounts of water.

On the behavioral side, learning to think before using water and correcting misuse can yield substantial savings. The bathroom, which accounts for 65 to 75 percent of the water used inside the home, is a perfect place to start making modifications. Depending on your showerhead, reducing a daily shower from ten to five minutes can save between 5,475 and 19,250 gallons of water a year. The average person can save 14,235 gallons of water annually just by turning the water off while lathering up in the shower, washing hands and brushing teeth. Outside the home, water use may constitute 50 to 70 percent of all residential water use during peak months. Using a broom instead of a hose to clear sidewalks, driveways and patios can save more than 100 gallons of water per use since a hose outputs about 50 gallons of water every five minutes.

"I hear and I forget. I see and I believe. I do and I understand." **Confucius**

Getting Around

Americans drive more and more each year. In the past forty-five years, vehicle miles traveled in this country has quadrupled, far outpacing population growth.[9] Nationally, the transportation sector is responsible for one-third of all man-made carbon dioxide emissions[10] and consumes 67 percent of all U.S. petroleum.[11] Taking all this into account, Americans' dependence and reliance on the automobile is an eminent contributor to congestion, sprawl, water pollution due to hard-surface runoff, atmospheric greenhouse gases and the extraction of oil from sensitive wild places.

Breaking the driving habit and establishing new routines such as consolidating trips, carpooling, using public transportation and biking or walking when traveling short distances can do more good for your community and the environment than just about anything else you typically do in a day. The average person, by driving two days less each week, can save about 143 gallons of gasoline and keep about 2,778 pounds of CO_2 out of the atmosphere in a year.[12] If only 1 percent of all licensed drivers followed suit, 273 million gallons of gasoline and 5.3 billion pounds of CO_2 could be saved this year.

Doing your share to embrace and popularize public transportation, ride sharing, biking and walking as alternatives to driving alone will set an example for other travelers as well as foster investment in viable mass transit and nonmotorized infrastructures. The advantages to discovering and utilizing transportation alternatives aren't just to the environment either. Rethinking all your uses of the car may reveal not only occasions to leave it at home, but also chances to improve your quality of life by reducing stress associated with driving hazards, long commutes, traffic congestion and parking aggravations.

Meat and the Environment

Each year Americans consume more than 200 pounds of meat and poultry per person,[13] but most meat-eaters are not aware of the staggering environmental impacts of raising animals for food—in particular, factory-style animal agriculture in which overcrowded conditions intensify the spread of disease, use of antibiotics, inhumane treatment of the animals and rapid degradation of implicated land and water sources.

The most basic flaw in producing meat for human consumption rests in the colossal waste and inefficiencies compared to producing other food sources. Pound for pound, far more resources go to produce meat than non-feed grains, fruits and vegetables. To produce one pound of beef protein takes vastly more water, land and energy than to produce one pound of vegetable protein. In fact, more than half of all water, one-third of fossil fuels used in the United States, and 87 percent of our agricultural land is devoted to raising animals for food.[14] The effects are not small. Water reserves in the West are being rapidly depleted. Energy-intensive farming practices have increased agricultural-related air pollution, acid rain, smog and greenhouse gases. Overgrazing is responsible for driving native plants, grasses and wildlife to the endangered list, degrading water quality, and compacting and eroding soil.[15]

Another problem is the nearly 1.4 billion tons of solid manure produced by U.S. farm animals per year—130 times the amount produced by the human population.[16] Runoff and seeping of more waste than the land can handle, and spills and leaks from huge waste lagoons, has led to the pollution of at least 39,750 miles of rivers and streams, and at least 943,560 acres of lakes and wetlands.[17]

In the final analysis, reducing or giving up meat and poultry consumption could improve the environment on a number of levels.

PURCHASING

The temptation and impetus to spend is all around us, and Americans on the whole are voracious consumers—out-consuming any other industrial nation per capita. In 2003, the economy was pumped up by more than 4.7 trillion dollars in consumer expenditures.[18] Our consumptive culture takes a heavy toll on the environment. Keeping up with consumer demand engenders the exploitation of scarce and fragile natural resources, huge amounts of toxic industrial emissions and discharges to air and water, the explosive growth of oversized retailers sprawled out across once-open or wooded land, and a waste stream bloated with excess packaging and discarded products and materials. The choice of a wide variety of goods, services and brands in a free market is a privilege and a responsibility. Abused, this privilege exacerbates environmental decline, but exercised responsibly, consumer choice can minimize the impact of purchases on the environment and in turn play a role in reforming amoral capitalism and protecting our ecological, social and economic systems.

In a capitalistic society, it is the consumer who decides what gets made and who gets to make it merely by giving or withholding their support. A consumer movement towards more nonmaterial spending and the purchase of natural and sustainable products can assist the growth of markets that are based on securing a better world. In the face of such burgeoning demand, emulous businesses and entrepreneurs won't be able to resist competing for a share of this market: the end result will be more earth-wise products and businesses to take the place of those that fail to regard sustainability goals and the shift in consumer preferences. In fact, it's already happening. The sustainable products industry is one of the fastest growing industries worldwide. However, in order to turn the tide on current consumer trends, more must be done to understand the link between purchases and the environment and to support companies that respect the earth and deliver sustainable solutions.

LINKING PURCHASES AND THEIR IMPACTS

Purchases of both necessity and extravagance, and everything in between, can have profound environmental impacts. Products can impact the environment in their extraction, manufacture, packaging, delivery, end-use and disposal—leaving a trail of environmental pollution and degradation reaching across continents. If it is your intention to support sustainability and cause less harm to the environment, you must seek to understand the connection between purchases and the environment and follow through with greener purchasing habits. Consider the following examples that illustrate the environmental benefits of lower-impact

buying decisions in three categories: paper, lighting and automobiles.

Completing the Recycling Loop

Everyone knows that the objective of recycling is to divert perfectly usable and valuable material from landfills or incinerators and to avoid exploiting virgin materials where recycled materials can be substituted. But recycling doesn't work just because you make a deposit to your recycling center each week. It takes consumers buying products made from recycled materials for recycling to fulfill its objective.

In the case of paper, the average American uses over 700 pounds of it each year,[19] and more than 90 percent of the printing and writing paper made in the United States is from virgin tree fiber—nearly half of all logged trees.[20] Even though recycled fibers eventually wear out and virgin sources for paper will always be part of the paper equation, the excessive and unnecessary consumption of virgin tree paper prevents recycled paper markets from reaching their potential (the current national paper recycling rate is approximately 43 percent) and increases pressure to overharvest forests.

> "Everyone thinks of changing the world, but no one thinks of changing himself." **Leo Tolstoy**

Switching to recycled paper would yield substantial environmental benefits: to make a ton of virgin paper requires between two and three-and-a-half tons of trees (roughly seventeen mature trees) compared to a ton of recycled paper that can be made from an equal amount (one ton) of recycled stock.[21] Manufacturing recycled paper also conserves substantial amounts of water and energy and produces less water and air pollution than making paper from virgin wood pulp.[22]

What a Difference a Kilowatt Makes

The process of generating electricity is the single largest source of industrial carbon dioxide emissions (the primary greenhouse gas) in the United States at 39.4 percent.[23] Consumers use far more electricity than is needed to live comfortably and safely, but running appliances less frequently and turning lights off when not in use are only part of the solution. Greater efficiency can be effortlessly achieved through the purchase and use of products that conserve energy in their use or rely on renewable resources for power.

For example, home lighting only accounts for about 10 percent of residential energy use, yet simple, corrective modifications in this area can easily save billions of pounds of greenhouse gas emissions and save the consumer money. If every household in the United States replaced incandescent bulbs with fluorescent bulbs in just one room in their home, the nation would save more than 800 billion kilowatts of energy and keep one trillion pounds of greenhouse gases out of the air. The energy savings would be equivalent to the annual output of more than twenty power plants.[24] Fluorescent and compact fluorescent lamps are more expensive than incandescent bulbs, but because they last six to ten times longer and save energy, they save the consumer money in the long run.

Outdoor lighting provides safety but becomes a source of waste when homeowners forget to turn lights off during the day. There are different products that can solve the problem. You can purchase outdoor lights with sensors that come on only after dark and only when they detect motion or heat, making sure they are in use only when needed. Solar-powered lights powered by small photovoltaic (PV) modules that convert sunlight directly into electricity, completely eliminate the misuse of energy from nonrenewable sources.

One of Your Biggest Purchases

When you buy a car, you are making a transportation decision that will repeat itself every time you start-up the engine. Gas mileage, or fuel economy, is a primary indicator of a vehicle's impact on the environment. Every gallon of gasoline burned emits 19.5 pounds of carbon dioxide into the atmosphere, so buying the most fuel-efficient car that meets your needs and budget is one of the best purchases you can make for the environment.

Since fuel-inefficient sport utility vehicles (SUVs) account for one of every four vehicles sold today and make up an increasing portion of miles traveled, their particular impact is noteworthy. SUVs use 33 percent more gas per mile driven than the average car today and emit as much as three times more smog-forming air pollution. In unexaggerated terms, their popularity has increased our reliance on oil, raised levels of the greenhouse gas carbon dioxide and fouled urban air.

Near the other end of the spectrum are hybrid electric vehicles (HEVs). HEVs consume significantly less fuel than vehicles powered by gasoline alone. The Toyota Prius gets up to sixty miles to the gallon[25] and its greenhouse gas emissions are less and exhaust gas cleaner—by up to 50 percent and 90 percent respectively—compared to the average 2004 vehicle.[26]

A NEW PURCHASING PARADIGM

The solution to reversing the "too much, too soon, at any cost" consumer culture in this country will require the steady adoption of new consumptive behaviors that include buying less and developing an awareness of and allegiance to companies and products that don't needlessly harm the environment.

Buying less entails not only resisting what you don't need, but also accepting a more conservative appraisal of what you do need. Although most people would probably say they shun superfluous spending, examples in American culture are all too common: building a house for four that can accommodate twice that number; buying a vehicle that suits the needs of an explorer; furnishing a home with more TVs than there are occupants; choosing one-use, disposable incarnations of consumer products; and filling your tank with high-octane gas when the car owner's manual recommends regular.

Consumer decisions should not be based solely on what is desirable, affordable and allowable. Before acting on buying impulses or familiar buying patterns, first give thoughtful consideration to the impacts of excess and inferior product criterion. Whether faced with a necessary purchase or a rare indulgent one, acquire knowledge about the products you intend to buy. What materials or ingredients make up the product? How did its creation or harvest impact the environment? Will its use and disposal aggravate or alleviate waste and pollution? *Chapter 4: Buying Green* has more information and guidelines on purchasing and understanding product labels; and *Chapter 5: Green Shopping Online* will assist you in finding earth-friendly alternatives to conventional products online.

CONSUMERISM, CAPITALISM AND THE ECONOMY

While many Americans admit that much of our consumption is gratuitous, they also see that spending is necessary for a strong economy. More than a few of our fellow Americans are adamant that satisfying every consumer urge is a national right that should not be interfered with. Consumerism may be a freedom and advantage of American culture, but current trends and practices are eroding long-term economic sustainability for short-term gains.

Overzealous and indiscriminant consumerism has brought about exploitative, unsustainable, and polluting industrial and agricultural activities that are undermining not only our environment but our economic future as well. The economic outlook of individuals, governments and businesses alike, tends to be dangerously shortsighted. Nothing could be worse for long-term economic stability than damaging, degrading and depleting the natural resources essential for producing food and rudimentary goods. Vegetation,

soil, fisheries, water, metals, fuels—without exception—are all being rapidly depleted.

Take the examples of the state of our fisheries and arable land base: the demise of world fisheries due to overfishing and the pollution and destruction of marine habitat threatens hundreds of millions of jobs and billions in revenue. And the United States will likely lose $40 billion from the export of food by 2030 due to the urbanization of farmland and loss of topsoil.[27] Likewise, participating in, sanctioning or otherwise assisting the dismantling of our forests today to manipulate immediate economic gains will have a devastating ripple effect as the unhealthy forests that remain fail to deliver on their ecological or economic welfare in the foreseeable future.

These examples point to one conclusion—vital resources and their capital, upon which we depend to sustain us and a healthy economy, can only be sustained through moderate consumption that supports a way of doing business that verifiably embodies sustainable resource management and waste and pollution prevention. Any business that operates differently is a liability to the environment, the public and the economy. Unfortunately, not all business leaders look far enough into the future to see the error of their ways. For this group, only a swift and dramatic decline in consumer loyalty and sales is likely to motivate corrective business modeling; and this fact gives ordinary consumers both the power and the responsibility to reform the marketplace through controlled, selective and thoughtful purchasing. Refuse to buy toxic and unsustainable products, and the corporations that offer them to us must either change or disappear. Consumers can learn to identify and choose to support companies that place a priority on bringing products to market and delivering services that minimize damage to the environment. Supporting businesses that take care of the environment and steadfastly rejecting those that do not will enlighten conventional businesses while enabling green businesses to prosper. By seeking out and purchasing more earth-friendly alternatives, consumers are letting manufacturers, growers and service people know that they want eco-responsible products and business ethics— and more of them.

TAKING ACTION

State and federal governments write the bills and pass the laws that constitute environmental policy. Influence that drives their agendas comes not only from constituents and peers; industry and special interest groups pay lobbyists large sums of money to bend legislators to their will. Often that means relaxing environmental regulations or seeing that they are excluded from new laws altogether, leaving us and the environment vulnerable. The rareness of voluntary

protection of the environment by industry and big business, and the often inadequate environmental policy and/or enforcement that allows poor management and exploitation of our forest, agricultural and marine resources, has led to the need for persistent public input on matters of corporate misdeeds and unabashed government leniency. Americans, by the millions, must insist on corporate accountability and demand that government policy support sustainable management of our resources and protection of the environment.

An added affront to environmental protection comes by way of large, unregulated "soft money" financial contributions to federal candidates (soft money contributions fall outside the regulatory limits on direct donations to federal candidates). Many believe such contributions have corrupted our government to the point where special-interest donors expect and receive favors in return for their contributions. When these favors aim to weaken basic environmental protections, they become a liability for taxpayers and much worse.

The lack of proactive protection on the part of big business and what is happening on Capitol Hill every day should be a wake-up call. Our voice is needed to reform corporations, take back control of our government from special interests, and restore common sense and ethics to people in the position to do great harm or great good.

> "The penalty good people pay for not being interested in politics is to be governed by people worse than themselves." **Plato**

EMPOWERING BUSY PEOPLE

The Internet has spawned a new and liberating form of activism referred to as "electronic activism." Electronic activism is convenient, fast and ideal for busy people who want to influence public or corporate policy on their coffee break. The mechanisms of this modern form of activism include action alerts (bulletins explaining the need for public support or protest of a particular deed); a menu of actions to choose from (popular choices include signing a pre-written petition or letter); and finally, the delivery of a communication to an intended audience (via e-mail, fax or U.S. mail).

From getting environmental news to sending letters to Washington, D.C., and CEOs, awareness and activism are being facilitated by the Internet. Organizations like Natural Resource Defense Council, World Wildlife Fund, Sierra Club, and no less than 100 others offer news bulletins to e-mail subscribers and provide opportunities to take a prescribed action in as little as five minutes. It's now quick and easy to learn and respond when the environment's well-being is threatened. Learn more about the efficiency and simplicity of taking action via the Internet in *Chapter 6: Getting Involved.*

GET OUT AND VOTE

Voting, an American right and duty, is not regarded as activism, although it can achieve similar results. Voting gives us a voice in who will form policy that affects our lives and environment, yet in the last presidential election, only 60 percent of eligible voters turned out to participate.

To the chagrin of many, voting can mean choosing between two or more unappealing candidates—vote anyway. Voting asserts that you are an active constituent, meaning your comments and opinions will be given more weight by delegates should you write to them during their term. Also, even if your vote is for the "lesser of two evils," you're still providing a valuable civic service by trying to deny the most dreadful candidate a seat in office!

When it comes to evaluating candidates running for public office, accurate information is critically important. Unfortunately, politicians and popular media (including television and radio) churn out mud-slinging ads, air misleading sound bites, report half truths and innuendoes, and present oversimplified arguments. Yet, not enough people recognize the diminished integrity of the media. According to a study conducted by the Center for Survey Research and Analysis at the University of Connecticut for the Radio and Television News Directors Foundation, most Americans continue to rely on and trust television for political news and analysis. But voting is too important not to look elsewhere for more truthful and less sensational commentaries. Organizations like Project Vote Smart (*vote-smart.org*) and League of Conservation Voters (*lcv.org*) report issue positions and incumbents' voting records instead of interpreting sound bites and campaign rhetoric.

Once you put someone in office, you have given them great power over you and your countrymen, so before making a choice for any candidate, make sure you know where they stand on issues that are important to you and the nation. Once in office, it could be years before they will be replaced. In the interim, you will have to live with their ethics, philosophies, loyalties, convictions and decisions.

CHAPTER 3:
ECO-TIPS FOR LIVING GREENER

Every day we may make a hundred or more choices, some small and seemingly insignificant, and some large and unquestionably substantial. Small or large, our collective choices and the actions that stem from them have an impact—good, bad or indifferent—on the world around us.

We all share responsibility for the health and sustainability of the natural world. We rely on the natural world for subsistence and survival and revere it for its power and beauty, yet it is declining—precipitously so—due to idle guardianship. Protecting the small and large environments where we live is not only sensible, it is essential. We all need to be more thoughtful in all that we do if we are to avoid a lifestyle of one mistake after another, and that means knowing and thinking about the consequences of the chores, routines, habits and activities that fill our days. Greener living will require examining and modifying some of our long-standing living patterns in order to refrain from or curtail activities that are needlessly harmful to the environment and to replace bad behaviors with better ones.

This chapter provides specific and effective tips for reducing your impact on the environment, but more than that, it is a tool of empowerment; by following instructions in this chapter, you can make improvements and make them stick.

Line dries GARMENTS

KILLER DESIGNER JACKET, bought used for $25

Antique ENGAGEMENT RING

LAPTOP, TELECOMMUTES 2 days a week!

DOESN'T BUY individual CDs, 1000 songs on one memory stick!

ALWAYS picks up PET WASTE

COMFY SHOES, runs errands ON FOOT!

KEEPING IT SIMPLE

The primary objective of this chapter is to provide practical tips that modern, busy people can use. Although limiting bathing to once a week and eating a diet of raw, vegan foods would certainly reduce your ecological footprint, suggestions are limited to those that have a higher probability of being adopted for the long term.

At first glance some tips may not appear so simple, but don't let up-front tasks prevent you from implementing changes that will simplify your life. Making recycling easier at home will require some planning and work. Finding suitable containers for recyclables and placing them, either in an existing space or one you have custom built, will require an investment in time that fits the type of collection system you want to create. Once completed, however, recycling at home will be neat, efficient and effortless.

Likewise, don't let up-front costs deter you either. A shower curtain made of hemp—a natural fiber and long-lasting alternative to plastic—can run about $75. However, this cost is less than the cost of replacing cheap plastic shower curtains and curtain liners, which can add up to hundreds of dollars over time. Investing in quality and durability will save the earth's resources and save you money.

As for those tips that are quite simple, simple doesn't mean unimportant. Even the simplest actions can make a difference when multiplied by many. If just 2 percent of the U.S. population turned on the kitchen and bathroom faucets to a fraction of full blast when washing their hands, nearly 12 million gallons of water could be saved every day. And if just 1 percent of the U.S. population used pot covers when cooking as opposed to not, we'd save about 14.6 billion British Thermal Units (BTUs) a day.[1] Don't make the mistake of underestimating the implications of small changes that are executed several million times a day by lots of others besides just you.

Your approach to, and follow-through on, these tips should be slow and steady. Positive changes are more likely to take hold and endure if you pursue one change at a time and pursue change deliberately. Following that prescription, choose just one tip from this list and take your time with it; "nurture" it until you understand it, become comfortable with it, and finally, commit to it.

When it comes to tips that address daily activities, there is no timetable and no deadline for their resolution. Whether it takes you one week or five to learn how, for example, to make two-sided copies at work and remember each time to do so, doesn't matter. What matters is that you take every bit as much time as you need to change your thinking and develop a routine. If new behaviors are to become learned behaviors and learned behaviors are to become habitual behaviors, then you must give yourself sufficient time to get used to doing something differently.

With respect to some tips, a slow and steady plan of action has limits. When it comes to tips that are seasonal or situational, you may have a narrow window in which to apply them. If you intend to reduce the amount of gifts exchanged within the family at Christmas, you'll need to address the subject and get agreement from everyone early in the season. Choose seasonal and situational tips when they are appropriate and execute them in a timely and purposeful manner.

WHAT ARE ALL THOSE BOXES FOR?

Working from right to left, use the boxes to note the following:

Tips you want to target

The tip you're currently working on

Your success with each tip-on a scale of 1 to 5

Start by reading through the tips at your leisure. When you're ready, begin to place checks next to the tips that interest you most.

You'll have the most fun with tips that you gravitate to first—a good place to start! The first check will enable you to quickly reference your favorite tips each time you revisit this chapter.

Once you've selected a set of tips that interest you most, read through them again with the purpose of choosing one with which to start. Once you've made your choice, place a check in the second box next to that tip.

Choose only one tip at a time so you can give it your undivided attention. With this one tip in mind, over the next several days you should begin to reflect on it, prepare for it (if necessary), try it out, practice it—whatever is required to see it put into effect.

Modifying behavior is not just a process of time; it's a process of application. So, keep applying what you've learned until a new behavior becomes a matter of course. Once you've carried out a tip suggestion and committed to the continued use of it, you're ready to move on to another, but not before you register your results in the third and final box. Your success with tips usually won't be pass/fail. You will probably achieve varying degrees of success given the nature of the tip and personal circumstances. Rate your success on a scale of "1" (not so good) to "5" (well done), and enter this number in the third and final box.

By recording a numerical "grade," you can recall at a glance which tips you may need or want to revisit at a later time to give it another go.

Once you've achieved resolution with the tips you initially selected, you can review the entire list of tips to focus on appropriate seasonal or situational ones or to find tips for which you have a newfound affinity. Your interests and resolve will grow as you learn more and start to put successes behind you, and tips previously overlooked may hold new meaning or have new application.

WHAT YOU NEED TO BRING TO THE TABLE

This chapter supplies ample suggestions and ideas for the person interested in greening their life. Although these tips express reasonable and achievable modifications, change requires flexibility and commitment. You must be willing to give what you learn here a fair chance, and that means sticking with it. Give yourself both the time and latitude to ride out the highs and lows of behavior modification. Expect bumps in the road, and get back on track as soon as you can. Speedy resolution is inconsequential, but staying the course is imperative for achieving results. Your reward for following through on these tips will be knowing that you're doing the right thing and making a difference.

THE TIPS
AT WORK

☐☐☐

Ask your employer to consider implementing a policy for compressed work weeks and/or telecommuting. Working four ten-hour days or working from home one or more days a week reduces commuting and traffic, leading to fewer toxic automobile emissions.

☐☐☐

Are you shopping around for a new computer? Consider buying a laptop. Laptops use 50 percent of the energy used by a typical desktop PC when plugged in and just 1 percent of the energy when running on batteries. (See resources under *Office and School Supplies* in chapter 5.)

☐☐☐

If your copier, printer and fax have a sleep or stand-by mode, make sure it is selected. From the sleep mode, it will automatically wake up when you go to use it.

☐☐☐

When using the copier at work, always make two-sided copies. If your printer also has a double-sided feature, use it.

☐☐☐

To print double-sided documents on a printer that has no double-sided feature, after selecting "Print," select "Print: Odd Pages," then "Send to Printer." Once all odd pages have come out of the printer, replace these pages in the paper feed tray so that the printer will print on the back/blank side of the paper. Return to your computer and now select "Print: Even Pages."

☐☐☐

At work, before you recycle paper, turn it blank side up (if it has one) and place it in a skinny three-ring binder or on a clipboard. Use this, instead of a new pad, for all note taking.

☐☐☐

Avoid using an extra page as a cover sheet by using the special "fax sticky notes" when faxing hard-copy documents.

☐☐☐

To save on paper, use disks to save work you've generated on your computer. If you're using your hard drive for this, that is fine too. Disks are good for backup though, in case your hard drive crashes. (See resources under *Office and School Supplies* in chapter 5.)

☐☐☐

If your office provides disposable cups for beverages, eliminate the need for them by bringing in extra glasses and mugs from home. Post a note in the lunch/break room requesting that your coworkers do the same.

☐☐☐

Lights should be turned off in unoccupied conference rooms and offices. If you walk by an empty conference room, switch the light off. Turn lights off in your own office when you'll be gone for more than ten minutes.

☐☐☐

Always distribute documents created on the computer via e-mails instead of via hard copy when it is professional and acceptable to do so.

☐☐☐

Recycle your empty printer, copier and fax cartridges. Empty laser and inkjet cartridges can be refilled or remanufactured several times. Businesses that collect, remanufacture and resell empty cartridges are easy to find. Look in the phone book under "Computer Supplies and Parts" or "Office Supplies." You can also go online—try ***aaaenvironmentalinc.com*** or ***tonerbuyer.com***. There are more resources listed under *Office and School Supplies* in chapter 5.

☐☐☐

Use suppliers that will take back their hazardous, recyclable or reusable products at the end of their life for proper disposal, recycling or remanufacturing.

BATHROOM

☐☐☐

If you have a nonconserving toilet (a 3.5 gallon flush or greater), retrofit the toilet with a water-saving device. There are several options that you can discuss with your local hardware professional, but an easy and quick fix involves placing one or two weighted bottles in the toilet tank to displace water flushed. Fill one-quart plastic beverage bottles with water for each nonconserving toilet in your home, and submerge first one, then two if necessary, inside each toilet tank. With each flush you will save water equal to the amount you've displaced, and thousands of gallons a year. *Note:* Be sure the bottle does not interfere with the operating parts.

"Never discourage anyone who continually makes progress, no matter how slow." **Plato**

☐☐☐

Replace your older toilets with an ultra-low flush model that will save several gallons of water per flush. The average home will save up to 17,500 gallons of water a year. *Note:* New innovations in low-flush technology have improved performance since it first hit the market.

☐☐☐

Fix all leaks. In fact, leaks waste so much water that you should check for leaks. To check for leaks, turn off all water in the house. Next, read your water meter, wait one hour (make sure no water is turned on during this period), and read the meter again. If the meter does not read exactly the same, there is a leak. Fixing leaks you can identify may be as simple as replacing a washer or tightening a connection. If you do have to hire a plumber to locate and/or fix a leak, the money will be offset by the savings on your water bill.

☐☐☐

Report tap leaks and faulty toilets in public places to management, so they can be fixed.

☐☐☐

Take short showers. With water flowing up to five gallons per minute from a nonconserving showerhead, showers consume about one-fifth of water used indoors.

☐☐☐

To save water in the shower, turn the water off while you lather up. If you're handy, you may want to install a water-control valve on your showerhead. The advantage of a valve is that it keeps the water (hot and cold) mixed while shut off.

□□□

Turn off the water while brushing your teeth or shaving. Running the water continuously for just two minutes can waste three gallons of water! Fill a cup with water when brushing your teeth and fill the sink bowl to rinse your razor instead of running the water.

□□□

Install water-saving devices in the bathroom if your fixtures are nonconserving. Faucet aerators and low-flow regulators for showerheads can reduce water output by 40 and 50 percent, respectively, while still delivering a satisfactory spray.

□□□

Avoid using your toilet as a wastebasket. Keep a trash can in the bathroom, but if you forget and toss garbage in the toilet bowl, leave it—it will eventually get flushed with normal use.

□□□

Buy a shower curtain that will far outlast cheap plastic ones; a shower curtain made of hemp will naturally resist mildew and is machine washable. (See resources under *Department Stores* in chapter 5.)

□□□

Use a strainer on all drains to catch hair and prevent drain clogs. If you do get a clog, use a metal snake to work the clog loose (available at hardware stores for around $12), not toxic drain cleaners.

Even though it is preferable to use a durable, mildew-resistant hemp shower curtain in place of a vinyl one, many still rely on vinyl. You can take the following steps to get the longest life out of a vinyl curtain:

- Stretch the curtain closed completely after a shower to eliminate folds where moisture cannot easily evaporate.
- Open the bathroom door and a window, if possible, after exiting the shower to allow steam to dissipate.
- Run the exhaust fan for five minutes following a shower.

Fix slow drains. Pour half a cup of baking soda down the drain and follow it with half a cup of white vinegar. Let it sit for twenty minutes to a half hour, then pour boiling water down the drain (about two quarts).

Turn your soap-bar scraps into usable shavings. Using a cheese grater, grate several scraps into shavings and put them in a decorative bowl next to the sink. Just take a pinch from the bowl with a dry hand, add water and work into a lather.

BUILDING AND HOME IMPROVEMENT

If you are planning to build a new home, think smaller. Smaller homes are more efficient and because they have to be planned more creatively to account for traffic patterns, space and storage, they can be much more architecturally interesting than larger structures.

☐☐☐

Carefully dismantle rooms and buildings during a renovation to salvage reusable materials and fixtures. To donate or sell what you salvage, check your phone book under "Building Materials—Used" or "Salvage."

☐☐☐

If you are building or renovating a home, check out salvage yards and antiques stores for used building materials and fixtures. They can be a great source of inexpensive and vintage items.

☐☐☐

If you are building a new home, you will lower your heating or cooling bills by choosing a site that is synergistic with the climate and weather patterns. Direct southern exposure is preferable in a cooler climate, but a shaded lot would be better in a very hot climate.

☐☐☐

If you live in a cold climate, paint your house a dark color. Dark colors reflect as little as 3 percent of sunlight, thus absorbing more heat. If you live in a warm climate, paint your house a light color that will reflect up to 90 percent of sunlight and keep your house cooler.

☐☐☐

Use water-based paints instead of oil-based paints. Water-based paint is less hazardous, dries faster, saves time and eliminates the need for chemical solvents for cleanup. (See resources under *Home Improvement* in chapter 5.)

☐☐☐

Reduce pollution from paint application by using brushes and rollers instead of sprayers. If you are determined to use a sprayer, use a High-Volume/Low-Pressure (HVLP) spray gun. As the name suggests, a high volume of air at low pressure is used to atomize paint and this reduces overspray and improves transfer efficiency. These guns are capable of a transfer efficiency of 65 percent or greater.

☐☐☐

Before discarding empty latex paint cans, leave the top off and allow the remaining paint to dry completely. Latex paint is not hazardous once it is solidified.

☐☐☐

Source green building materials. Choosing lower-impact products for home-improvement projects can reduce toxins in the home and environment, reduce waste and preserve natural resources. (See resources under *Home Improvement* in chapter 5 and under *Building and Home Improvement* in chapter 7.)

☐☐☐

If you have leftover paint, save it for a future use. Properly sealed and stored, paint will last for years. Just clean the lip of the can thoroughly, secure the lid tightly, and store the paint can upside down to create a tight seal around the lid and keep the paint fresh until you need it again. If you cannot clean the lip and lid thoroughly, transfer paint to glass jars. Finally, store your paint in a cool place, but where it won't freeze. Even when you can't use it or don't want it anymore, leftover paint can be donated.

☐☐☐

Use wool floor coverings instead of synthetic alternatives; they are more durable and easier to clean. Wool can be expensive, though. Find bargains on wool carpet by looking through remnants at local carpet outlets. Remnants are often marked down by as much as 60 percent or more and the sizes can be adequate to carpet an average room—or have the edges bound to create an area rug.

CLEANING AND LAUNDRY

☐☐☐

Save old, tattered towels and T-shirts for cleaning. Cut them into squares and they become useful rags that can replace store-bought rags and paper towels.

☐☐☐

Use oxygen- or hydrogen-based bleaches instead of chlorine bleach, which is very harmful when released into the environment. (See resources under *Cleaning* in chapter 5.)

☐☐☐

Use reusable and durable cleaning instruments such as cotton washrags and natural-bristle brushes instead of one-use wipes and cheap supermarket sponges.

Reduce your risk of exposure to toxic chemicals by reading the packaging on products to find these statements: nontoxic, biodegradable, chlorine-free, phosphate-free, non-petroleum based, vegetable oil based, fragrance-free and no dyes. (See resources under *Cleaning* in chapter 5.)

Make your own household cleaners. This is a safer alternative to relying on harsh, toxic commercial products. Effective cleaning products can be made with borax, washing soda, distilled white vinegar, baking soda, salt, club soda, cooking oil and lemons. On their own or combined together, you can make scouring powder, furniture polish, an all-purpose cleaner and more! (See resources under *Green Cleaning* in chapter 7.)

Instead of running the water while cleaning, fill a bucket with water and a general-purpose cleaner and scrub down sinks and showers completely before rinsing. To rinse shower walls, fill a watering can with water and pour water along the top of the walls, letting the water wash away soap and grime.

Buy products in concentrate when available. You'll use less, making your cost per use much lower than it would be with a non-concentrated brand, and you'll be consuming less packaging.

Buy a front-loading washing machine; they are far superior to top loaders for saving water and energy.

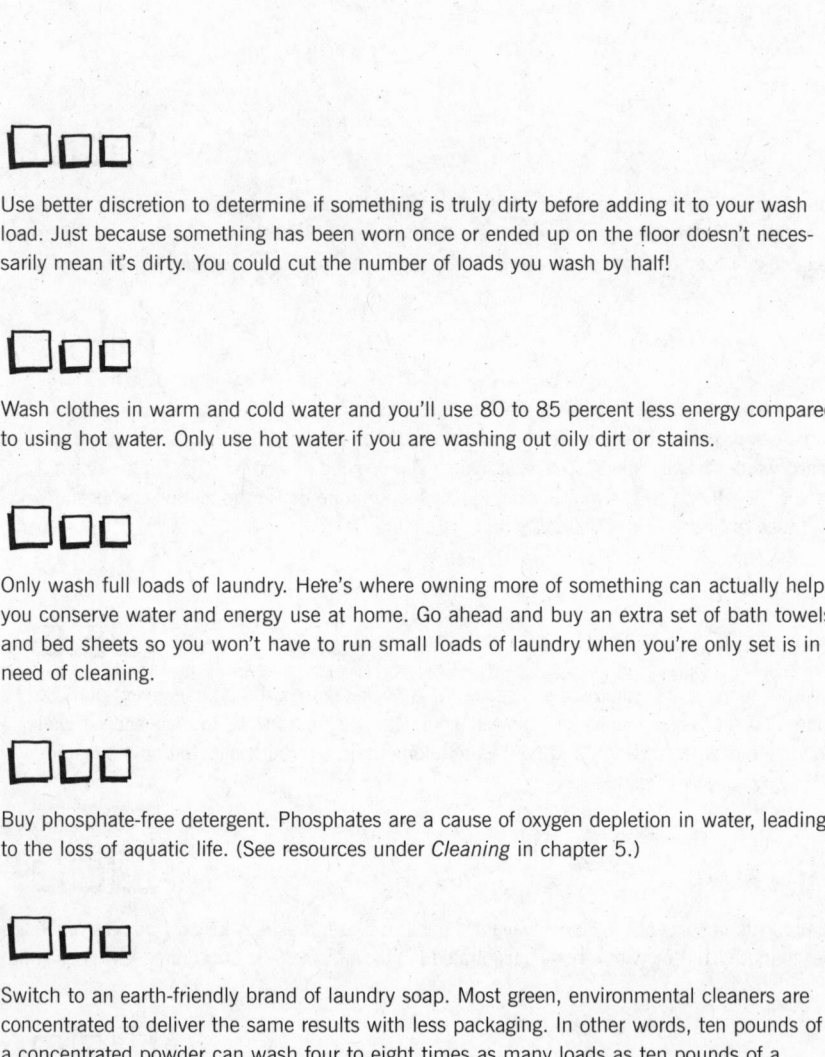

☐☐☐

Use better discretion to determine if something is truly dirty before adding it to your wash load. Just because something has been worn once or ended up on the floor doesn't necessarily mean it's dirty. You could cut the number of loads you wash by half!

☐☐☐

Wash clothes in warm and cold water and you'll use 80 to 85 percent less energy compared to using hot water. Only use hot water if you are washing out oily dirt or stains.

☐☐☐

Only wash full loads of laundry. Here's where owning more of something can actually help you conserve water and energy use at home. Go ahead and buy an extra set of bath towels and bed sheets so you won't have to run small loads of laundry when you're only set is in need of cleaning.

☐☐☐

Buy phosphate-free detergent. Phosphates are a cause of oxygen depletion in water, leading to the loss of aquatic life. (See resources under *Cleaning* in chapter 5.)

☐☐☐

Switch to an earth-friendly brand of laundry soap. Most green, environmental cleaners are concentrated to deliver the same results with less packaging. In other words, ten pounds of a concentrated powder can wash four to eight times as many loads as ten pounds of a non-concentrated powder.

"You must be the change you wish to see in the world." **Mahatma Gandhi**

☐☐☐

Buy a dryer with a moisture sensor setting. The dryer will automatically shut off when the clothes are dry, saving energy and wear and tear on your clothes.

☐☐☐

Use a drying rack for delicate or lightweight items. Items that can and should be air-dried include lightweight synthetics, wool, silk and wool/silk blend fabrics. Diverting such fabrics from the dryer will help lighten dryer loads for more rapid drying and extend the life of fabrics that will air-dry overnight.

☐☐☐

Use professional wet cleaning instead of dry cleaning. Most dry cleaners use perchloroethylene (PERC) to clean clothes and it is toxic. Wet cleaning has been used on fabrics such as wool, linen, silk and rayon with excellent results, and wet cleaning prices are the same as for dry cleaning.

☐☐☐

Line dry your sheets in warm months. If you've got two trees in your back or side yard, you can string up a clothesline in minutes.

ENERGY

☐☐☐

Keep your refrigerator full. Food retains cold better than air does, so a near-empty fridge is working much harder to cool its contents. Don't overstuff your fridge either. Air circulation is needed to cool and control humidity.

☐☐☐

Your refrigerator should be set close to 37 degrees Fahrenheit and your freezer set to 3 degrees Fahrenheit to conserve energy. Place a weather thermometer inside the compartment to check its temperature and adjust the dials until you achieve the desired temperature.

☐☐☐

Clean refrigerator gaskets regularly and vacuum the condenser coils twice a year. Your refrigerator will operate more efficiently and use less electricity.

☐☐☐

Wrap your water heater in an insulating jacket if it is located in an unheated space such as a basement or garage.

☐☐☐

Use your microwave. Cooking and reheating with a microwave is faster and more efficient than using the stovetop or oven, thus reducing up to 70 percent of energy use.

☐☐☐

Use a toaster oven for small jobs. It will use a third to half as much energy as a full-size oven.

☐☐☐

Turn off the oven ten to fifteen minutes before cooking time runs out; food will continue to cook without using the extra electricity.

☐☐☐

If you own a dishwasher with a booster heater, make sure it is turned on. Using the booster heater heats the water at the source, so you can set your hot-water tank to a lower temperature (about 120 degrees Fahrenheit). If you're unsure if your model has one, contact the manufacturer.

☐☐☐

If you have a "no-heat" dry setting on your dishwasher, use it. Heat drying is not necessary after a hot-wash cycle. If you don't have an air-dry setting on your model, turn the dishwasher off after the final rinse and prop the door open, allowing your dishes to air-dry.

☐☐☐

Shift appliance use to off-peak hours. Off-peak hours are typically from 9 p.m. to 7 a.m. Your utility company may also offer off-peak energy rates, in which case you can save money by running appliances during lower-rate periods. Call your utility company to find out if they offer off-peak rates and during what times.

☐☐☐

Arrange furniture to take advantage of natural light from windows. Place desks and reading chairs next to windows to cut down on the need and use of supplemental, artificial light during the day.

☐☐☐

Install dimmer switches where dimmed lighting makes sense, like the dining room and hallways. Dimming a light by 25 percent saves an equal percentage of energy.

☐☐☐

Switch to fluorescent bulbs in areas where extended lighting is required. Though the initial price is higher than for incandescent bulbs, fluorescent lights produce four times as much light per watt, last up to ten times as long and therefore cost one-third as much to operate.

☐☐☐

Reduce the number of bulbs in linear light fixtures that give off more light than you need. Or replace some bulbs with lower-watt bulbs to conserve energy.

☐☐☐

Paint interior walls a light color to reflect light. If you decorate with dark walls, at night, use task lighting to avoid using too many peripheral lights.

Turn off all lights when not in use. If you're worried about running into obstacles while feeling for light switches, invest in some fluorescent night-lights to illuminate halls and rooms just enough to locate switches safely.

Install a motion sensor on lights in stairwells or on dark landings where light is needed only when passing through.

Turn off exterior lights in the morning. Better yet, use a timer or install motion detectors so the lights will only come on when they are needed.

Use an outdoor compact fluorescent light (CFL) that is between 9 and 18 watts if you are lighting outdoor areas for security. A CFL, which does not shine as bright as an incandescent flood spot, will save energy and actually permit better visibility into dark areas that aren't illuminated than brighter floods permit.

Schedule an energy audit to learn more about your energy consumption and what steps you can take to cut energy costs. Many utility companies and service providers perform energy audits at no or low cost to you.

☐☐☐

Install ceiling fans to save money on cooling and heating and reduce energy waste. In the summer, use them in place of a central air conditioner. In the winter, a ceiling fan with a motor that runs in reverse can push warm air down from the ceiling and thus conserve energy.

☐☐☐

Run heat-producing appliances such as washers, dryers, dishwashers and ovens during the cooler hours of the day in the summer months.

☐☐☐

Don't place lamps with incandescent bulbs near your air-conditioning thermostat. The heat given off by them will register on the thermostat, causing the air conditioner to run longer than necessary.

☐☐☐

Set central air-conditioning units as high as is comfortable. For each degree above 78, you'll save 6 to 8 percent in cooling costs.

☐☐☐

Keep windows and drapes closed on hot days to reduce radiant solar gain.

☐☐☐

If you are heating an outdoor pool, cover your pool at night to conserve 40 to 70 percent of energy that would otherwise go up in steam.

"That which we persist in doing becomes easier for us to do; not that the nature of the thing itself is changed, but that our power to do is increased."
Ralph Waldo Emerson

☐☐☐

Check air conditioner filters; they should be cleaned or replaced monthly to help the unit run at peak efficiency. If you have an outdoor unit, make sure its coils are unobstructed by debris, plants or shrubs.

☐☐☐

In hot climates, block or filter direct sunlight into your home by shading windows on the south and west sides of the house with awnings, trees or shrubs.

☐☐☐

Set your thermostat no higher than 68 degrees in winter. This is a very comfortable temperature if you are dressed properly.

☐☐☐

Take extra steps to maximize heating efficiency when the weather turns cold.
- Close shades and curtains to reduce heat loss as soon as the sun goes down.
- Open all the shades and curtains during the day, except those on north-facing windows, to take advantage of solar heat gain.
- Close doors and vents to rooms that are not being used.

☐☐☐

Install a thermostat that can be programmed to turn down the heat at bedtime, and turn it back up just before you wake in the morning. This could save you up to 20 percent on heating costs.

☐☐☐

Make sure your furnace is working at peak efficiency. One simple thing you can do is clean or replace the filter monthly or as needed.

☐☐☐

Apply door sweeps to the bottom of exterior doors and install weather stripping to minimize gaps and thus heat loss.

☐☐☐

When shopping for new appliances, look for those equipped with energy-efficient standby power devices that use one watt or less of energy per hour. Without these devices, appliances can draw four to seven watts per hour even when unused, and the Department of Energy estimates that approximately twenty-six power plants are needed just to power these so-called "energy vampires."

☐☐☐

Change the setting of the power-saving feature on your computer so that during periods of inactivity, your computer shuts down the monitor at five minutes, the hard drive at thirty minutes, and finally puts the computer in sleep mode at thirty-five minutes.

☐☐☐

Purchase Tradable Renewable Energy Certificates (TRCs) or "green tags." More renewable electricity is generated and delivered into the regional power pool, thus displacing an equal amount of other conventional electricity generation, such as coal, oil, and large hydro or natural gas. To learn more, see resources under *Energy* in chapter 7.

Learn how to make an efficient and clean fire in your fireplace by following these steps:
1. Loosely crumple newspaper (uncolored) on the floor of the firebox. Use less if your kindling is fine and dry, more if the opposite is the case.
2. Place finely split, dry kindling on top of and behind the paper. Top it off with two to three small pieces of firewood.
3. Open all air controls and light the newspaper in several places to achieve rapid ignition. Then, quickly close the "front door" halfway to create a strong draft. In seconds, you'll have a bright, hot fire.
4. To this, add several small pieces of firewood, being careful not to smother the fire.

Note: These suggestions are general guidelines and apply to many wood-burning systems. However, consult your operation manual for special firing techniques that may be required for your system.

Use an electric, propane or natural gas grill instead of burning charcoal or wood briquettes, which produce harmful smoke when burned. *Note:* If your electricity comes from coal-burning power plants, avoid an electric grill.

HAZARDOUS WASTE

Become familiar with what common household items contain potentially hazardous ingredients, and then take steps to find nonhazardous alternatives. For a list of common household products with potentially hazardous ingredients, see resources under *Green Cleaning* in chapter 7.

☐ ☐ ☐

Use a small garbage can in your garage to dispose of hazardous waste in their original containers. When it becomes full, take it to a hazardous waste treatment center.

☐ ☐ ☐

Dispose of expired medicines by calling your pharmacy or local hospital to find out if they have a collection stand from which a company picks up expired medicine and sees to its safe disposal or destruction. If neither do, contact your local hazardous waste disposal center for instructions.

HOLIDAYS

☐ ☐ ☐

Limit the number of gifts you buy for people. Pick a single family member's name out of a hat and give a gift only to that person. Also, suggest a gift theme of earth-friendly gifts that won't harm the environment.

☐ ☐ ☐

Choose gifts that support reuse. Visit local antiques shops where you can find some real treasures that are bargains too.

☐ ☐ ☐

Give gifts that don't come with a lot of packaging or require wrapping. Examples include event tickets, gift certificates, money and memberships.

Give the ultimate nonmaterial gift for Christmas this year—your time and/or talent. Examples include:

- Baby-sitting or pet-sitting
- Granting a special favor
- Teaching another a skill you have which they have always admired and wanted to learn
- A date including tickets to a special event or performance

Give your holiday a different meaning and focus: start traditions that don't center around gift giving, like annual game tournaments, cook-offs, book discussions, craft sessions, etc. These activities can still center around family and a traditional feast, while providing more joy and fulfillment than a material gift.

Buy gift wrap made from recycled paper. If your store does not sell recycled gift wrap, ask them to please stock it in the future. (See resources under *Paper Products* in chapter 5.)

Save used wrapping paper for next year. Save boxes that collapse, bows, ribbons and gift bags too. When it's time to recycle wrapping paper, make sure the paper is recyclable. If you're not sure, check with your local recycling company for guidelines.

Instead of buying wrapping paper to wrap gifts, use materials from around the house that can serve as gift wrap. Root out and use any of the following for earth-friendly wrapping:

- Old posters and maps
- Old sheet music
- Wallpaper scraps
- Scarves and pillowcases
- Fabric remnants
- Colorful ads or photos torn out of magazines and catalogs

Minimize wrapping this year by choosing an alternative way to present your gifts. Here are some ideas:

- Many of the paper carrying bags you get from stores during the holiday shopping season are festive enough to double as gift bags.
- If you purchase an item that comes in a large box, place it under the tree on Christmas Eve and drape a scarf or throw blanket over it.
- Clothing items can be rolled and tied in the middle with a wide silk ribbon.
- Small items, such as a necklace, can be stuck deep in the Christmas tree. On Christmas morning, make the recipient search among the branches for their gift.
- Items for the house can be placed where they will eventually be kept and used with just a bow and card attached. Throughout the day, the recipient will discover their gifts.

Buy a permanent tree instead of a disposable one. An artificial tree will last a lifetime.

Recycle your Christmas tree within the first week after December 25th, so you don't miss the chance. Mulching, chipping or composting Christmas trees after the holidays is an earth-wise alternative to throwing them into landfills. In many counties, for a limited time following Christmas, trees will be picked up for recycling if left at the curb. Call your recycling company for details. Remove all trimmings before taking the tree from your home. If your community doesn't provide Christmas tree recycling services, visit *gardenweb.com* for ideas on how to use your discarded tree at home.

Buy a living Christmas tree to transplant in your yard. This can be a good option for anyone with the desire, space and climate to transplant live trees in January. A live tree should remain inside for no longer than three to five days, and placed in a cool room that is free of hot or cold drafts. Transplanting a tree in December/January is risky, so consult a local nursery before choosing a live tree.

Use less energy for holiday lights by following these tips:
- Choose strings with fewer bulbs and the fewest watts per bulb.
- Choose LED lights, which are more energy efficient than incandescent ones.
- Operate your lights for no more than four hours a night and use a programmable timer so they will not accidentally remain on overnight.

Note: LED lights may be hard to find locally. To purchase online, visit *ledup.com, realgoods.com* or *giftsfourseasons.com/ledlighting.html.*

Make your own gift tags out of last year's Christmas cards by cutting out the design on the card.

☐☐☐

Send the fronts of holiday greeting cards you receive to St. Jude's Ranch for Children. The children in St. Jude's care make and sell new cards from the old ones they receive. Mail card fronts to *St. Jude's Ranch for Children, 100 St. Jude's Street, P.O. Box 60100, Boulder City, Nevada, 89006.*

KITCHEN/MEALS

☐☐☐

Buy organic foods. Organic farms use natural growing practices that promote sustainable agriculture and provide healthy alternatives to conventional crops grown with pesticides and genetically modified organisms. Ask your grocer's produce manager to stock organic produce.

☐☐☐

Seek out local farmers' markets and buy locally grown, seasonal produce to cut down on environmental costs associated with transporting produce to your community from great distances. (See resources under *Safe Food and Sustainable Agriculture* in chapter 7.)

☐☐☐

Eat less meat. Reducing your meat consumption would reduce food-related land use and water pollution problems.

☐☐☐

Purchase a water-filtration system if you're concerned about your drinking water, instead of relying on bottled water.

☐☐☐

Buy fish that are not caught or farmed in ways that harm the environment. (See resources under *Safe Food and Sustainable Agriculture* in chapter 7.)

☐☐☐

Reuse glass jars for food storage. Plastic food tubs, such as those used for yogurt, can also be reused. (See guidelines for reusing plastic in this chapter under *Reduce/Reuse/Recycle*.) For larger portions of leftovers, use soup and mixing bowls, then fit the top with a saucer or plate in place of plastic wrap.

☐☐☐

Buy several cloth napkins and use them instead of paper at home and on the go. Cloth napkins can be used several times before washing. Give each family member a unique napkin ring to store their napkin between meals.

☐☐☐

Use a reusable hemp or gold coffee filter instead of paper coffee filters, or make filterless coffee with a french press.

☐☐☐

When ordering takeout, take steps to reduce the waste it will produce. If you're taking it home, don't take what you won't need (e.g., napkins, flatware, etc.). If the food is being delivered, ask your order-taker to write "NO NAPKINS, FLATWARE OR CONDIMENTS" directly on the order ticket.

☐☐☐

Fill a bowl with cold water and wash fruit and vegetables this way, instead of letting water from a faucet run over them.

☐☐☐

Make sure the kitchen faucet is in the "cold" position when turning it on for brief periods. You'll waste significant energy turning on the hot water even before hot water starts to flow.

☐☐☐

Install a tankless, instant water heater inside the cabinet under your kitchen sink if your hot-water tank is located some distance from your kitchen, and you typically have to run the water a long time before it turns hot. This will save considerable water and energy.

☐☐☐

Store a pitcher or bottle with water in the refrigerator instead of running the kitchen faucet until the water runs cold enough for you to drink.

☐☐☐

Turn the faucet on at a fraction of full volume for things like washing hands and rinsing dishes to save considerable water.

☐☐☐

Cut back on or stop using single-serving and single-use products that consume needless extra paper and plastic for packaging.

"The reward of a thing well done is to have done it."
Ralph Waldo Emerson

☐☐☐

Reuse water leftover after common household uses to water plants instead of pouring it down the drain (e.g., from a double boiler, washing produce, steaming vegetables, cooking pasta, soaking beans, soaking frozen meat in its packaging, etc.). Transfer leftover water to a watering can for later use. Make sure water is cool before using it to water plants.

☐☐☐

Buy in bulk whenever possible, thus avoiding the excess packaging that comes from buying smaller quantities.

☐☐☐

Cook in bulk when you can to store away future lunches in reusable containers. Packing leftovers to work or school means you can avoid takeout and all its packaging.

☐☐☐

Use the dishwasher only for full loads for the most efficient water use. If you have a small number of dishes or pans to clean, wash them by hand. You'll save the most water by filling a basin with just three to four inches of water, stacking the dishes as you wash them, and then rinsing them quickly under a light stream of water.

☐☐☐

If your dishwasher can handle it, scrape but don't rinse dishes before putting them in the dishwasher. If dishes do have to be rinsed first, try to rinse them immediately after preparing food or eating—before food has had a chance to harden.

☐☐☐

Always cover pots when cooking. It speeds up cooking and uses less energy.

☐☐☐

Patronize restaurants that practice water conservation, such as by serving water only upon request. If you do go to a restaurant that automatically serves water and you do not want it, upon being seated, turn your water glass upside down before they have a chance to fill it. If they bring full glasses of water to the table, politely refuse them and ask if they can use them at another table.

☐☐☐

Let hot foods cool before putting them away in the refrigerator so as not to raise the internal temperature. *Note:* The USDA cautions not to leave meat, poultry or egg products out for longer than one hour. Place these leftovers in shallow containers so they will cool more quickly.

☐☐☐

Compost scraps from your kitchen to produce rich humus for your garden. To learn more about composting, see resources under *Gardening and Lawn Care* in chapter 7.

LAWN AND GARDEN

☐☐☐

Make sure your garden hose is adapted with a trigger nozzle and that any leaks are patched with a hose mender. *Note:* If you need a hose mender, note the size of your hose (inside diameter) before leaving for the hardware store; hose menders come in different sizes.

Don't use a hose to clear dirt and leaves out of the garage or off sidewalks, driveways and patios. Use a broom to conserve water.

If it's okay in your area, install rain gutters and rain barrels to collect rainwater from your roof for use in your garden and for other chores like washing the car. (See resources under *Outdoors/Lawn and Garden* in chapter 5.) Using collected rainwater eliminates the wasteful use of potable water for outside chores and protects waterways from excessive storm-water runoff.

Eliminate mosquito breeding grounds by making sure there is no standing water on your property. Check and empty trays beneath flower pots, rain gutters, barrels, pails, bird feeders, etc. This will cut down on the need to use repellants.

Install a bat house to control mosquito populations effectively and naturally. A single bat can eat up to 1,000 mosquitoes a night. (See resources under *Gardening and Lawn Care* in chapter 7.)

Avoid planting too much lawn. Lawns need lots of water and provide no habitat for local wildlife. Create a meadow of indigenous wildflowers, plant an attractive ground cover, or plant an organic herb and vegetable garden instead. Consult your local extension office (normally affiliated with a college or university) for guidance.

☐☐☐

Check the weather forecast before automatically watering your lawn. There could be rain in the forecast.

☐☐☐

Never water with a sprinkler on a windy day. Wind will carry away much of the water before it hits the ground.

☐☐☐

Adjust sprinkler heads and water flow as best you can to avoid "watering" hard surfaces and structures.

☐☐☐

Soak your lawn no more than once a week or every five days to encourage deep root growth and a healthy lawn. In the hottest and driest of conditions, this amount of watering will not prevent a lawn from going dormant and turning brown, but the solution is not to overwater. This is natural and your lawn will rebound when cooler temperatures and rain return.

☐☐☐

If you don't have an automatic irrigation system, and you rely upon a moveable sprinkler to water, purchase a timer for your hose bib(s) that will allow you to program when the sprinkler comes on and shuts off. In the interim, set a cooking timer or alarm clock inside the house to remind you to move the sprinkler or to turn off the water.

If you live in a dry climate, try xeriscaping. It's a water-efficient approach to landscaping and can save 30 to 50 percent on water use. (See resources under *Gardening and Lawn Care* in chapter 7.)

Plant native grasses, plants, trees and shrubs in your yard. Since they are adapted to local insect species and weather, they won't require extra watering or pesticides. Your local nursery can help you select species.

Water your yard or garden in the early morning or evening when it is cooler. This will discourage excessive evaporation.

Use soaker hoses or drip irrigation in gardens; they provide accurate, deep watering for your plants that will encourage strong root growth.

Wash your car on the lawn, not in the driveway or street. The rinse water will water the lawn and be diverted from storm drains. Make sure you use an earth-friendly, biodegradable soap and use it sparingly. Or, take your car to a car wash that collects and recycles its rinse water.

☐☐☐

Use an electric or chimney briquette starter on charcoal, not lighter fluid, to reduce the toxins emitted from outdoor cookouts.

☐☐☐

Choose human-powered lawn and garden equipment if you can get the job done without gas-fueled equipment. For larger jobs, electric equipment may also be substituted. (See resources under *Outdoors/Lawn and Garden* in chapter 5.)

☐☐☐

Compost your leaves and yard trimmings and divert compostable material from overburdened landfills. If you don't have room to compost on your property, take yard waste to a local yard debris recycler. Call your local transfer station or dump to inquire.

☐☐☐

Protect land you own from unwanted development. Join a land trust and create a conservation easement to ensure permanent protection for specified land. There are over 1,400 local and regional land trusts across the country. To find one, see resources under *Livable Communities* in chapter 7.

REDUCE/REUSE/RECYCLE

☐☐☐

Buy products of quality that will last a long time. Avoid buying products that are made cheaply, to be used once and then disposed.

Buy rechargeable batteries and a battery charger. Most rechargeable batteries can be recharged up to 1,000 times.

Replace alkaline batteries in portable devices with rechargeable NiCd, NiMH or Lithium-ion batteries. Check with the manufacturer on compatibility.

Recycle rechargeable batteries that no longer hold a charge. Find the nearest battery drop-off location by going to *rbrc.org* online or by calling *1-800-8-BATTERY.*

Discharge rechargeable NiCd or NiMH batteries completely before recharging. Recharging these types of batteries when only partially depleted can damage them, leading to more frequent replacement. Go to *greenbatteries.com* to learn about the different types of rechargeable batteries and to purchase batteries and chargers.

Take worn-out rechargeable battery packs for cordless tools and appliances to a merchant that can rebuild the battery. To find such a merchant, look under "Batteries" in the phone book.

☐☐☐

Upgrade old computers with new memory, microprocessors and drives. Or donate them to a computer refurbisher or recycler. Do not let them end up in a landfill where their toxic materials can pose environmental hazards. To locate recycling and reuse organizations, see resources under *Reduce, Reuse and Recycle* in chapter 7.

☐☐☐

Never throw a cell phone into the trash—see that it gets reused or recycled. Cell phones have a toxic waste stream including lead, mercury and cadmium. When discarded improperly, these toxins are released into the environment. To find out how to recycle your unwanted cell phone, see resources under *Reduce, Reuse and Recycle* in chapter 7.

☐☐☐

Buy a paper shredder and use it to shred nonrecyclable paper. Then use the shredded paper as packing material.

☐☐☐

Cut worn-out clothes, bedding and towels into squares and use the pieces as cleaning rags, handkerchiefs or napkins.

☐☐☐

Use old and worn-out clothing, sheets, bedspreads and drapes for sewing projects. If you're not crafty or haven't the need, donate clean items to a sewing or quilting group.

☐☐☐

Recycle worn-out athletic shoes. Nike will take your worn-out athletic shoes and turn them into Nike Grind—a material used in sports surfaces. For details, go to **nike.com/nikebiz/nikebiz.jhtml?page=27.**

☐☐☐

Check out books from the library instead of buying them. Try to buy only books you will read, lend and refer to several times over your lifetime. If you are somewhat of a collector and like to own books, shop used booksellers.

☐☐☐

Donate used art supplies to a local school or day care center.

☐☐☐

Borrow or rent items if you have only a temporary or occasional need for them instead of purchasing, if at all possible.

☐☐☐

Donate working, useful items to a local charity.

☐☐☐

Open an account at a consignment shop for nice things you want to get rid of. There are shops for specific items, such as CDs, clothes or furniture, as well as stores that sell a wide range of merchandise. You'll make a commission if the store sells your items.

☐☐☐

Use crumpled newspaper as packing material instead of polystyrene foam (such as Styrofoam) peanuts. The production of polystyrene depletes the ozone and it takes several hundred years to degrade in a landfill. Divert just enough newspaper from your recycle pile so that you'll have adequate packing material on hand when you need it.

☐☐☐

If you receive a shipment packed in plastic peanuts, locate a shipping company in your area that will take them off your hands. The Plastic Loose Fill Council operates a searchable online database and a toll-free number so anyone can find the closest drop-off location where leftover plastic packing peanuts are reused. Go to *loosefillpackaging.com* online or call the Peanut Hotline at *1-800-828-2214.*

☐☐☐

Donate empty egg cartons to a local egg producer. Sometimes you can make the donation through the store that sold you the eggs.

☐☐☐

Try joint ownership with family, friends or neighbors of large or expensive things that receive only periodic use (e.g., lawn mower, chain saw, snowblower, power tools, car ramps, etc.).

☐☐☐

Share equipment and tools that you own with trustworthy friends and family.

☐☐☐

Purchase antique or estate jewelry instead of new. The mining of precious metals and gems in many countries has been the source of environmental degradation, political turmoil and human rights violations. When it comes to used jewelry, you are not tied to the design or setting. You can reset stones or recast metal to update the jewelry.

☐☐☐

Get off mailing lists that send you unsolicited CDs. It just takes a quick phone call to do so.

☐☐☐

Download software online directly to your computer hard drive instead of buying software on CD.

☐☐☐

Invest in a digital audio recorder that can store various hours of audio recordings on a memory stick. Download music online and never buy individual CDs again!

☐☐☐

Subscribe to your cable or satellite provider's service that feeds movies directly to your TV "on demand," instead of purchasing movies on DVD.

☐☐☐

Buy a thermos mug or ceramic mug and keep one at work and/or in the car. Every time you visit your favorite coffeehouse, use that mug instead of the paper or polystyrene cups they provide.

Reuse or recycle unwanted media products in the following ways:
- Donate CDs and DVDs to a charity thrift store, library or day care.
- Sell them to a reuse store or pawnshop.
- Trade them or give them away to friends and family.
- Recycle them into new media products. See resources under *Reduce, Reuse and Recycle* in chapter 7.

Get off mailing lists you don't want to be on. To learn how, see resources under *Reduce, Reuse and Recycle* in chapter 7.

When asked to choose between paper and plastic bags, say "neither." Buy durable cloth bags and take them on all your shopping trips—not just to the grocery store. Keep some in the car or in your carry-all at all times so you won't be without them when you need them. (See resources under *Reusable Bags* in chapter 5.)

Always stop and think before automatically considering a broken item garbage. If an object you own is beyond repair, you may be able to do some dismantling and salvage parts to reuse yourself or to recycle, donate or sell. For example, the wheels and handle from a broken push lawn mower can be reused in building a wagon for a child or to assist in yard chores. A broken broom handle can be used as a plant stake, walking stick or hanging rod. Steel and aluminum parts from a busted bike can be recycled. Get into the habit of looking at broken things differently and with the goal of diverting as much as possible from the waste stream.

Say "no thanks" to a bag if you don't really need one. Retail checkers are too quick to bag items that do not require one. If you are buying only a few items, refuse a bag and carry them out.

If you haven't gotten around to buying reusable cloth shopping bags, reuse your paper or plastic bags several times before finding another household use for them or recycling them where possible.

When buying plastic containers, try to buy those that are labeled with a 1 or 2 within the chasing arrows symbol; these two types of plastic are widely recycled. Avoid buying plastics with numbers 3 through 7; they are difficult to recycle.

Reuse type 4 plastic bags as small wastebasket liners or to pick up pet waste. Make sure not to put these bags in the same collection bin as white HDPE number 2 plastic bags at the super-market—if your market has such a bin. These two plastics are incompatible.

Stash some cardboard boxes in your car and use these instead of bags at the grocery store. At checkout, reload groceries directly back into your shopping cart, then cart your groceries back to the car and load them into the boxes.

"Do something every day that you don't want to do; this is the golden rule for acquiring the habit of doing your duty without pain." **Mark Twain**

Reuse number 5 plastic food tubs and number 2 beverage bottles when it is appropriate. An appropriate reuse would be a new use that is consistent with its original use and adheres to any limitations set by the manufacturer, which would be printed on the container. Below are some of the finer details that will help you reuse plastic safely.

- Never microwave food in a plastic container. According to the FDA's article, "Plastics and the Microwave," substances used in plastic food containers can leach into food. The article goes on to state, "the amount of a substance expected to migrate into food and the toxicological concerns . . . [are] well within the margin of safety based on information available to the agency." If your personal tolerance is zero, use approved glass or ceramic in the microwave.
- Leaching is most likely to occur when plastic has aged, cracked (freezing can cause this) or comes in contact with fatty foods or heat.
- Always clean plastic containers with warm, soapy water between each use.
- If a reused container starts to show signs of deterioration (discoloration, cloudiness, scratches) recycle it, find a non-food use for it or throw it away.

Put larger produce items (e.g., oranges and peppers) directly into the grocery cart instead of using the small plastic bags provided. As for bags you do take, save them for reuse. Keep them stored in an old cereal box marked "Produce Bags" under the sink or in the pantry. Take the box with you to the store and reuse those bags for as long as they last. Bags used to bring home grains can also be reused for produce or grains again.

If you buy bottled drinking water, save empty bottles and refill them rather than recycling them and buying new bottles continuously. Many grocery stores now have filtered water vending machines where you can fill-up for about 30 cents per gallon.

☐☐☐

Wash out soiled plastic food-storage bags to get a few more uses out of them. This is an easy chore as long as you don't let bags pile up. Wash them two at a time as follows: Turn two bags inside out and slip your hands inside (like you are wearing gloves). Next, go through the act of washing your hands—only you'll be washing the inside of those bags instead. Rinse bags while still on hands, and then slip each bag (still inside out) over a tall bottle to air-dry.

☐☐☐

Use glass jars brought from home when shopping for certain food and nonfood items sold in bulk (e.g., peanut butter, maple syrup and dish soap). If your market provides plastic containers in their bulk section, ask the manager if you can use clean containers brought from home instead. You will need to have a jar weighed by customer service while it's empty, so that its weight (or tare) can be deducted upon checkout. If you are using like-sized jars, you only have to do this for one jar, one time. Thereafter, you can simply tell the cashier at checkout what the tare is. So you won't forget, mark the tare on jar lids in permanent ink.

☐☐☐

When buying packaged products, all other things being equal, buy the brand that uses the least amount of packaging.

☐☐☐

Share a magazine subscription with a friend and recycle issues when you're finished with them.

☐☐☐

Purchase mismatched dishes and flatware from a thrift store to use at outdoor cookouts and picnics in place of disposable wares.

☐☐☐

Send electronic greeting cards for appropriate occasions. There are several Web sites from which you can send personalized greetings to anyone with an e-mail address. Two Web sites that provide this service for free are **hallmark.com** and **cards.amazon.com.**

☐☐☐

Reuse cardboard boxes for shipping or moving. Large retailers discard hundreds of clean, sturdy boxes in all sizes every day. Recover what you need from their recycling depository at the back of the building.

☐☐☐

If you have recently moved to a new address, but still have several checks left with your old address, you do not necessarily need to order new checks. If your ID has been updated, in most cases you can continue to use the checks you still have. Just handwrite your new address and phone number on the checks as you write each one or affix new-address stickers.

☐☐☐

Use pawnshops to find computers, electronics, power tools, jewelry, household appliances, sporting equipment, musical instruments and more. *Note:* Once of dubious reputation, now the pawn industry is highly regulated.

☐☐☐

Reuse note cards that are missing their envelopes by tearing or cutting them in half down their spines and using the card fronts as postcards or index cards. Card backs with a blank side can also be used as index cards. This tip also applies to used cards with a blank inside or outside face. What cannot be salvaged for a new use can be recycled.

Soak labels off glass jars and reuse the jars around the house to organize loose items.

Make your own cold packs from reused plastic beverage bottles. Fill bottles a little less than full (to allow for expansion), cap them and place them in the freezer. Once the water inside is frozen solid, you'll have cold packs for your coolers! Use various sizes of bottles, depending on the size of your cooler and how long you want the ice to last.

Locate a photofinisher who sees to it that recyclable materials leftover after film processing are being collected and recycled. This can include plastic film canisters and lids, the magazine and spool from the film roll, and one-time-use cameras. There are also the following reuses for film canisters:

- In your sewing basket to hold pins and organize small novelties such as buttons, snaps, etc.
- At the office to organize small items in or on your desk such as loose change for vending machines, paper clips, mechanical pencil eraser refills, pushpins, etc.
- When traveling, as containers for face cream, extra razors, etc.
- On camping trips for matches. (Matches may have to be cut down to fit.)
- In the workshop for miscellaneous hardware such as washers, nuts, small screws, etc. Glue or tape one of the contents to the outside for identification.

Breathe new life into old furniture; have it repaired, refinished or reupholstered.

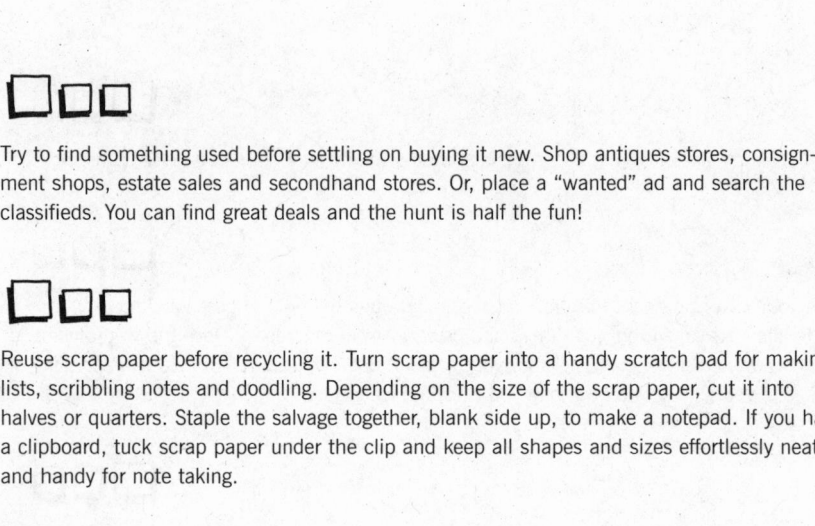

Try to find something used before settling on buying it new. Shop antiques stores, consignment shops, estate sales and secondhand stores. Or, place a "wanted" ad and search the classifieds. You can find great deals and the hunt is half the fun!

Reuse scrap paper before recycling it. Turn scrap paper into a handy scratch pad for making lists, scribbling notes and doodling. Depending on the size of the scrap paper, cut it into halves or quarters. Staple the salvage together, blank side up, to make a notepad. If you have a clipboard, tuck scrap paper under the clip and keep all shapes and sizes effortlessly neat and handy for note taking.

Use the reply envelopes you receive in unsolicited mailings for your own mailing needs. It is quite acceptable for casual mailings. When ready to use, ink over any preprinted bar codes, then affix an address label over the preprinted addresses.

Have a sufficient number of receptacles for recyclables, and a designated place for them, to make recycling much easier. Here are some suggestions for facilitating home recycling while keeping it tidy as well.
- Buy an eleven- to thirteen-gallon trash can (lid is optional) for each material you will be recycling and label them (e.g., GLASS, STEEL CANS, NEWSPAPER, etc.). If your city or county provides curbside collection, label receptacles according to how items must be sorted at the curb.
- Store the trash cans in a pantry, utility room or garage; the closer they are to your kitchen, the better. You may be able to place these receptacles directly at curbside if your community has curbside recycling.

☐☐☐

Take used motor oil to your local service station for recycling. Motor oil never wears out; it can be recycled, re-refined, and used again and again.

☐☐☐

Buy food packaged in paper, glass, aluminum or steel as often as you can. All these containers are readily recyclable. Avoid plastic: only 3.9 percent of all post-consumer plastic is being recycled today, and plastics as a percentage of the waste stream is rapidly growing.[2]

☐☐☐

Know what is recyclable within your community and buy products packaged accordingly. Call your local recycling center for a list of clear guidelines on what you can recycle. *Note:* Don't try to recycle items not approved by your recycler. The illicit material could contaminate an entire batch of recycling. A clean, sorted stream of materials is essential if recycling is to be economically viable.

☐☐☐

If your curbside recycler does not accept materials you know to be recyclable (e.g., mixed paper, magazines, paperboard, etc.), check with other area recyclers. You can stockpile these items in the garage and make a trip once a month to a regional recycling center that does accept them. (See resources under *Reduce, Reuse and Recycle* in chapter 7.)

☐☐☐

Get your news online and cancel newspaper subscriptions.

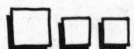

Plan to collect recyclables if having a party. You can achieve this very discretely by following these steps:

1. On the day of the party, empty two lower adjacent cabinets in the kitchen (take out removable shelves too).
2. Place empty cardboard boxes or bins inside the cabinets.
3. Make signs that indicate what is being collected (e.g., "GARBAGE" "ALUMINUM CANS", "GLASS", etc.), and tape the signs to the outside of the cabinet doors.

Receptacles will be neatly tucked away, yet your intention to recycle will be clear to your guests.

Call your local recycler for a list of contaminants you should avoid. Common contaminants include the following:

Used napkins and paper plates
Food residue
Waxed boxes
Labels on tin cans
Bottleneck rings
Metal lids or caps
Windows and mirrors (however they may be collected elsewhere for crushing and reuse in construction materials)
Pyrex and ceramics
Plastic wrap
Carbon paper
Foil gift wrap
Paper printed with metallic ink
Plastic-coated paper
Photographs

TRANSPORTATION

Commute to work by bicycle, if possible, or use an electric bike if distance, terrain or health mandates it. Electric bikes range in price from under $500 to $2,500 and can travel up to twenty-five miles on one charge. Get more information on electric bikes and scooters in chapter 5 under *Energy and Appliances.*

If your errands cover a three-mile radius, leave the car at home and ride your bike. A good backpack or pull cart makes transporting smaller things easy. If you can get to where you're going in twenty minutes or less on foot, walking is a better alternative to driving as well. Use good judgment and bike or walk only where it is safe to do so.

Turn your ignition off when you will be stopped or parked for more than thirty seconds. Idling for more than thirty seconds burns more gas than it takes to restart the engine or than if the car were moving, and thus produces more toxic emissions.

Use the lowest-octane gas recommended for your car. Only one in ten cars produced since 1982 require high-octane gasoline, and high-octane gasoline releases a higher concentration of toxic compounds into the air than the lowest octane gasoline.

Keep your vehicle tuned up. A well-tuned engine will conserve gas and reduce the toxic emissions produced by your engine.

"I am only one, but I am still one. I cannot do everything, but I can do something." **Helen Keller**

☐☐☐

Use car roof racks on an as-needed basis. Their use increases wind resistance, which increases fuel consumption. If you can transport stuff inside your vehicle, do so. And if you don't need your roof rack, remove it as soon as you can.

☐☐☐

Drive slower. For every mile per hour you drive under sixty-five miles per hour, you improve your car's fuel efficiency by about 2 percent. So, if you're driving fifty-five miles per hour, you increase you car's fuel efficiency by up to 20 percent!

☐☐☐

Check your tire pressure once a month and before long trips to keep tires at their optimal pressure for better gas mileage.

☐☐☐

Join a car-sharing network if you rarely need a car. It is a low-impact way to meet your occasional driving needs and you can save lots of money! See resources under *Transportation* in chapter 7.

☐☐☐

Consider only the most fuel-efficient cars when buying a new car. To find which cars are rated highest for fuel efficiency and low emissions, see resources under *Transportation* in chapter 7.

If you have more than one car, always drive the most fuel-efficient car when it is available to you.

Abandon your car in favor of cleaner transportation—at first just once a week, and later two to three times a week. As you adjust to new modes of transportation, you should be able to reduce the miles you drive by more than 50 percent. But don't stop there if you can reduce miles even further!

Avoid conventional antifreeze, which is highly toxic. Buy antifreeze made from propylene glycol, which is lower in toxins and biodegradable, or recycled antifreeze. As a last resort, you could buy an "extended life" product that will last for five years or 150,000 miles. It's toxic, but because you'll use less, it's preferable to conventional antifreeze, which generally has to be replaced every thirty months or 30,000 miles. Whichever antifreeze you choose, recycle it at the end of its useful life. Many auto repair shops will recycle antifreeze on-site, or remove the antifreeze and send it to another location for recycling.

Try public transportation for one week. There are considerable advantages to you as well as the environment.
- You can save on gas, maintenance costs, parking fees, parking tickets and possibly insurance premiums.
- You won't have to worry as much about accidents, vehicle wear and tear, vandalism or theft.
- You won't have to deal with tolls, traffic, bad drivers or parking.
- You can catch up on reading or pass the time with a hobby, like knitting, during the ride.

☐☐☐

Explore your carpool opportunities. Type up a notice stating you are interested in discussing carpooling and post it in approved areas at work, school or wherever you are commuting to. Make sure you pick your carpool buddies carefully; interview each candidate for personal, geographical and schedule compatibility.

☐☐☐

Use cleaner, renewable biodiesel in place of petroleum diesel in diesel engines. This can be done with little or no modifications to the engine, according to the National Biodiesel Board. Visit **biodiesel.org** to find pump stations and for recommendations for making a problem-free transition. *Note:* Any switch to a fuel that is not specifically recommended for your engine by its manufacturer should take place only after consultation with a qualified mechanic.

TRAVEL/RECREATION

☐☐☐

Book a trip to a destination that will benefit the local people and environment (see resources under *Travel and Recreation* in chapter 7) instead of vacationing in a destination that is often visited and overburdened by tourists.

☐☐☐

The next time you check into a hotel for more than a day, phone housekeeping upon your arrival and decline the housekeeping service. According to commercial laundry equipment manufacturers, foregoing fresh towels and bed linens can result in saving as much as thirty gallons of water per room per day.

Unplug appliances to save energy while you're away. Many small and large appliances continue to draw electricity even when turned off.

If your home will be vacant while you're traveling, turn down your thermostat in winter and up in summer to a temperature only necessary to protect houseplants or pets left behind.

Resist the temptation to take those small, complimentary bottles of shampoo and lotion provided by hotels home with you. The excess packaging used for such small quantities is extremely wasteful. If guests didn't use or take them, hotels would stop providing them.

Brochures or maps are commonly provided at tourist attractions. Take care of them and as you're leaving, return your brochure or map to the place from where you got it so someone else can use it.

When visiting a park, never leave paths (nor allow your children to) and do not disrupt or remove anything (e.g., rocks, flowers, etc.). Leave them for the next person and everyone after them to enjoy as you have. Most importantly, leave them for the species that depend upon them.

☐☐☐

When camping, protect campsite water sources from contamination by never washing dishes, clothes or yourself in them. Use a basin and a small amount of biodegradable soap for washing chores. Dump wastewater in a hole at least twenty-five yards from waterways.

☐☐☐

If you will be camping, leave the campsite and park better than you found it. Carry all trash out with you; do not burn or bury garbage of any kind, and check your campsite thoroughly to make sure nothing gets left behind.

☐☐☐

If you have an RV, camper van or other low-mpg recreational vehicle that you take on long trips, offset its gas usage and emissions by driving a ULEV (Ultra-Low Emissions Vehicle) for everyday driving and driving less when it makes sense.

☐☐☐

If you own a boat, protect the water by always using a funnel when refueling from a gas can. Be equally conscientious when refueling from a gas pump to avoid spills.

PETS AND ANIMALS

☐☐☐

Always pick up after your pet. The density of pets in urban neighborhoods combined with the fact that urban surfaces (including lawns) are hard, leads to significant runoff during heavy rain, causing bacterial contamination of urban water.

Order biodegradable pet waste bags (see resources under *Pet Products* in chapter 5). You can also use litter that you may find when out walking your pooch. Hopefully there is no litter where you walk, but if there is, you can solve two problems by picking up the litter (e.g., a snack bag or soda cup) and then using it to remove your pet's waste.

Don't feed waterfowl human food. It can harm them in the following ways:
- They become satiated by and dependent on the unhealthy food and stop foraging for natural plant and animal material.
- They lose their desire to migrate to warmer climates where natural food sources are abundant.
- The constant artificial food source contributes to overpopulation, resulting in water-quality concerns.

CHAPTER 4:
BUYING GREEN

Some of the biggest problems facing this planet stem from consumer choices. The electricity we buy, the car we drive and the food we eat make a difference because these choices, and so many like them, are not isolated. Assuring that what we buy, use and throw away won't cause needless or inordinate harm to the world around us requires learning more about the products we intend to buy—how their creation and use affect air and water quality, for example—and replacing un-eco buying habits with ones that are more ecologically sound.

The green consumer is thoughtful, restrained, assiduous and discerning when it comes to making buying decisions. These disciplines, and the knowledge to follow through on them, won't come overnight, and busy people should grant themselves the time to transition to greener buying habits by taking it one purchase at a time. Starting today, make an effort to learn more about the products you use and the companies behind them. Nothing less than a consumer movement that boycotts flagrant polluters, rejects excessive packaging, and seeks out nontoxic and sustainable alternatives will issue the directive to corporate America that their principles must be consistent with, not at odds with, environmental values. With such a movement, we will start to see technologies, practices, and products that defy and adulterate environmental and public health replaced by ones that respect them.

THE LAWS OF GREEN PURCHASING

The laws of green purchasing, in their most rigid forms, can best be summed up as "buy not, buy less, buy green." Assuming the choices you make won't endanger anyone or interfere with your obligations, this prescription is sound. Pursued absolutely, you would "buy not" if you could not justify a practical need for something, "buy less" when less would do, and "buy green" whenever possible.

Before deciding to buy anything nonessential, give it some serious thought. If you cannot come up with a useful and reasonable need for something, go without. Producing, using and eventually disposing of what is not really needed accelerates the depletion of finite natural resources; exacerbates industrial, commercial and municipal pollution; and expands the waste stream. Nevertheless, abstaining from all purchases that go beyond those required to sustain life and occupation, all be it prudent and noble, is also unrealistic. The temptation to make purchases that transcend our needs from time to time is inevitable. Life wouldn't be the same without the occasional indulgence for self and pleasure—the operative word being "occasional." Refraining, more often than not, from making superfluous purchases will go a long way in minimizing the effect our collective acquisitions have on the planet.

Once you've decided to buy something, the next step is to accurately assess how much you need. Always go with the smaller or least of something to satisfy your need. Whether you're buying home furnishings, a car, a new appliance or toys for the kids, buy consistent with practical requirements. Try not to buy based on a big budget, a product's image, the space you have at home or the pleadings of little voices. Every super-sized and unnecessary purchase adds up against the environment.

The final step in completing a greener purchasing decision is to choose the product that causes the least environmental harm. Products include the obvious tangibles like food, electronics, clothing and office supplies, and intangibles too, like vacation packages, utilities and country club memberships. And products are an integral part of services you may be in need of, like interior designing, event planning, day care, catering, housecleaning and lawn maintenance. One purchase at a time, start to acquire knowledge about the products and materials you intend to buy outright, and those you'll buy when choosing a particular service contractor.

"The more clearly we can focus our attention on the wonders and realities of the universe about us, the less taste we shall have for destruction."
Rachel Carson

WHAT IS A GREEN COMPANY OR PRODUCT?

"Green" is a generic term used to describe something that has a benign or moderate effect on the environment. Thus, it follows that a green product is one that causes less harm to the environment than other similar products. Environmental impacts arising from a product's many life cycle stages actually begin prior to manufacturing with the harvesting, extraction or processing of input materials. During manufacture, systemic effects emanate from energy usage, atmospheric emissions, and solid and waterborne waste discharges. Following manufacture, use and final disposal of a product may contribute the most lasting environmental impacts.

Whereas conventional product development tends to focus on price, performance and safety, green product development heeds these product considerations while also vigorously pursuing ways to improve a product's environmental impact across all stages of its life cycle.

The goals of a green producer or manufacturer include the following:
- Preserving natural resources and wildlife habitat
- Protecting air, water and soil quality
- Producing less toxic pollution and waste
- Maintaining land integrity and area
- Protecting animal welfare

Depending on the product, its environmental valuation can be assessed by considering the answers to some basic questions. Using the set of questions on page 96, you can determine a product's "greenness" by the number of times you can answer "yes" to questions that apply. Some answers will be readily apparent, others may take time and experience to become clear, and a few may never get answered to your satisfaction, but asking the questions of the products you'll need will, at the very least, approximate their "greenness," thereby helping you to avoid evidently less desirable choices. Helpful to your assessment as well will be product labels, which are discussed in the next section.

QUESTIONS TO ASK ABOUT A PRODUCT OR ITS MANUFACTURER

Is the product produced locally to minimize energy used for transport?

Was the product produced using organic growing methods, and is it in season?

Was it raised humanely and without supplemental drugs or artificial additives?

Does it come from readily renewable resources?

If it was made with natural resources, was extraction done responsibly without impairing wildlife habitat, water quality and resource sustainability?

Does it utilize recycled or reclaimed materials?

Is it made without toxic ingredients, thereby reducing the production and release of toxic/hazardous emissions?

During its manufacture, were efforts made to recovery materials for reuse or recycling to minimize solid and waterborne wastes?

Does the manufacturing plant utilize energy-saving systems and procedures for production operations?

Are pollution-control devices used and maintained to reduce poisonous and greenhouse gas emissions?

Is it packaged minimally or in recycled-content packaging?

Is it of good design and quality, made to last a long time?

Is it the most energy-efficient and clean (producing zero or low-atmospheric emissions) product of its kind available?

Is it adaptable and can its life be extended to meet changing needs and tastes through upgrading or refurbishing?

Can it be recycled or remanufactured at the end of its life?

Does the manufacturer accept responsibility for taking back the product for refurbishing or recycling at the end of its useful life? (This applies to resource and energy-intensive products that pose significant waste liabilities such as electronic products.)

"There is no shame in not knowing; the shame lies in not finding out."
Russian proverb

ECO-LABELS

The most obvious and likely place a consumer looks for product information is on its packaging—that being anything that's wrapped around, stuck on or attached to the product. Unfortunately, you can only partially rely on packaging for pertinent product information, because sometimes it's what packaging doesn't say that is most telling. Packaging can, however, provide useful information when a producer, by means of a label, can claim to be abstaining from an unfavorable process, practice or constituent and using beneficial ones in their place. In such cases, labels—either a marking or a descriptor—referred to as "eco-labels" serve to highlight a product's unique ecological benefits. A label can be (1) a defined and regulated/verified claim (e.g., "Organic"); (2) a defined, but unregulated/unverified claim (e.g., "Biodegradable"); or (3) an undefined and unregulated claim (e.g., "Eco-Safe").

Defined claims that are substantive and verified by a reputable third party provide the best assurances to consumers. Defined claims that are voluntary, and therefore not independently verified, have meaning but only to the extent that producers, manufacturers and distributors follow the law. Without oversight, there's always the chance that unethical businesses will seize the opportunity to deceive consumers.

An undefined claim is subjective and can mean anything the manufacturer wants it to mean. Claims like "Green," "Environmentally Preferable" and "Eco-Safe" have no standard definition. This doesn't mean all such claims are baseless, it only means that their meaning can be very inconsistent from manufacturer to manufacturer and product to product. The only way to know what an undefined claim means is to call the manufacturer and get more information. Those with nothing to hide won't mind providing you with honest, straightforward answers.

Regardless of whether a claim is defined and verified by a third party or undefined and unverified, Truth-in-Labeling laws apply. No manufacturer can legally defraud the public with false claims. Protect yourself by contacting a manufacturer if you are unfamiliar with an eco-label they are using. Ask the following pertinent questions:
1. What does the label mean?
2. Is there a second- or third-party organization or agency behind the label that is removed from the product it is certifying?
3. Are the label guidelines available for public review, and if so, by what means?

Labels may not be a perfect medium for learning all there is to know about a product, but at the point of purchase, it may be all you've got. All products, packaging and services impact the environment in some way, but some less than others;

reading labels will help you find those in the latter group as will becoming familiar with some basic product attributes that render products good choices for the environment. There are too many product labels and attributes–good, bad or indifferent–for the scope of this book, so the emphasis is on common labels of which a better understanding will help you become greener consumers.

Labels Legend
DR = Defined and Regulated
DU = Defined but Unregulated
UU = Undefined and Unregulated
A = Attribute
P = Pending

LABELS AND ATTRIBUTES AT A GLANCE

General
Biodegradable[DU]
Green[UU]
Green Seal[DR]
Natural[UU]
Reclaimed or Recovered[A]
Recyclable[DU]
Recycled[DU]
Reusable[A]
Used[A]

Food Products
Animal Care Certified[DR] (eggs)
Cage Free[DU] (eggs, poultry)
Dolphin Safe (tuna)[DR]
Free Farmed (dairy products, eggs, poultry, meat)[DR]
Free Range, Free Roaming or Pasture Raised[P] (beef, pork)
Free Range[DU] (poultry)
GMO Free or GE Free[DU]
Grass Fed[P]
No Antibiotics Used or Raised Without Antibiotics[DU] (dairy products, poultry, meat)
No Hormones Administered[UU,P] (beef)
Organic—Certified[DR]
Natural[DU] (meat and poultry)
NutriClean[DR]
Pesticide Free, No Pesticide Residue[UU]
rBGH Free or rBST Free[UU] (dairy)
Sustainable Fishery—Certified[DR]
Transitional[DR]

Energy/Power
Clean[UU]
Green[UU]
Green-e[DR]
Renewable[UU]

Cleaners and Solvents
Biodegradable[DU]
CFC Free[DU]
Chemical Free[UU]
Chlorine Free[UU] or Totally Chlorine Free—
   Certified[DR]
No or Low VOCs[UU]
Nontoxic[UU]
Ozone Safe or Ozone Friendly[DU]
Phosphate Free[UU]

Appliances, Home Electronics and Lighting
Energy Efficient[UU]
Energy Star Rated[DR]
LCD[A]
Refurbished or Remanufactured[UU]
Solar Powered[A]

Paper Products
Recycled[DU]
Tree Free[UU]
Sustainable Forestry—Certified[DR]
Chlorine Free,[UU] Totally Chlorine Free—
   Certified[DR]

Plastic Products
Recyclable[UU]
Recycled[UU]

Personal-Care Products
CFC Free[DU]
Chemical Free[UU]
Fluoride Free[UU]
Natural[UU]
No VOCs or Low VOCs[UU]
Organic—Certified[DR]
Ozone Safe or Ozone Friendly[DU]
Wildcrafted or Wildharvested—
   Unceritfied,[UU] —Certified[DR]

Textile Products
Green[UU]
Natural[UU]
Organic—Certified[DR]

Vehicles
Biodiesel[A]
Electric[A]
Fuel Cell Powered[A]
Fuel Efficient[UU]
Hybrid[A]
Low Emissions Vehicles[DU]

Wood Products
Composite[UU]
Reclaimed, Recovered or Salvaged[A]
Sustainable Forestry—Certified[DR]

THE FINE PRINT

Animal Care Certified Beware of this label sponsored by United Egg Producers— "animal care" seems of little concern to the authors of the label guidelines. They include allowing hens to be caged in an area smaller than a sheet of copy paper for their entire lives.

Biodegradable The Federal Trade Commission defines "Biodegradable" as a substance that has been scientifically proven to break down entirely and return to nature; i.e., decompose into elements found in nature within a reasonably short period of time after disposal.

Biodegradable (Cleaners and Solvents) Most detergents and soluble chemicals degrade in wastewater systems, but when they break down and what they break down into is what separates eco-friendly biodegradable liquids from the not so friendly. If you read "Biodegradable" on a package, keep reading. Look for indications that the product is also made up of nontoxic, renewable ingredients that will break down quickly without deleterious effects on the environment into which treated wastewater is discharged.

Biodegradable (Solids) Biodegradable products, although better than nonbiodegradable ones, still face serious impediments to decomposing in landfills.

To biodegrade, sunlight, air and water must be present, but by law, our landfills are designed to keep sunlight, air and moisture out, to avoid pollutants from the landfill entering the air and drinking water. Deprived of what they need to biodegrade, even food and paper can take decades to decompose in a landfill. Buy biodegradable products, but don't let this be the only thing you do to moderate persistent waste. Rely primarily on reduction, reuse, recycling and composting as a means of reducing solid waste.

Biodiesel An alternative fuel made from vegetable oil. (It is not raw vegetable oil.) Compared to diesel fuel, biodiesel is better for the environment because it is made with renewable resources, is nontoxic, biodegradable and has lower emissions.

Cage Free This label guarantees that chickens were not restrained in cages, but it does not guarantee that they spent any time outdoors.

CFC Free In 1977, chlorofluorocarbons (CFCs), the compounds that propelled aerosol products into the air and depleted the earth's protective ozone layer in the upper atmosphere, were banned in nearly all consumer products. Many aerosol products were reformulated with either Hydrochlorofluorocarbons (HCFCs) or hydrofluorocarbons (HFCs) propellants. HCFCs also deplete stratospheric ozone, but to a much lesser extent than CFCs. HFCs do not deplete the ozone; however, they evaporate when the product is sprayed and contribute to air pollution. To avoid fluorocarbon propellants, buy solid, liquid, gel, powder, pump and stick forms of products.

Chemical Free This is an arbitrary label, but in an effort to avoid exposure to harmful chemicals and to reduce their proliferation, seek out chemical-free products to the best of your ability. The U.S. government requires products containing toxic chemicals to carry the words "DANGER," "POISON," "WARNING" or "CAUTION," so reject products with such labels. Three thousand chemicals are used in high volume in the United States[1]—many of them untested by the EPA, and many of them known by their manufacturers to pose risks to humans and wildlife.

Chlorine Free Chlorine is a poisonous toxin and one of today's most heavily used chemical agents. Both chlorine and toxic by-products of the industrial use of chlorine, called organochlorines, are released into the environment every day, where they can combine with other molecules to form new toxins that accumulate and last for years. Manufacturers may only use the claim "Chlorine Free" if chlorine was not used during any stage of a product's manufac-ture. For third-party confirmation of a chlorine-free claim, look for the Chlorine Free Products Association's "Totally Chlorine Free" label.

Clean Energy "Clean"—although not a defined, regulated label—characterizes energy-generating technologies that release little or no air emissions. Clean energy sources include the sun (solar energy), wind, water (wave and small-scale hydro power), heat from the earth (geothermal energy), and hydrogen (pure hydrogen fuel cells). There is an abundance of these resources and the technology to harness and produce energy from them, yet only about 2 percent of our energy supply comes from the resources listed above. "Clean" energy only describes technologies that produce low emissions—it does not reveal ancillary environmental impacts, if any. Nuclear energy, for example, has been described as clean because its air emissions are fairly low, but nuclear power generation creates liabilities both in mining uranium and disposing of radioactive waste. And high-impact hydro power—generated by trapping river flows behind massive dams—another clean energy source, has flooded vast areas of land, endangered fisheries, and altered the water flow and quality of affected rivers. See also, *Renewable Energy*.

Composite Boards The composite boards consumers are most familiar with are those manufactured for decking applications. They are the result of bonding waste wood and other materials from industrial processes or post-consumer recycled materials. There are many "recipes" for composite boards and they range from very environmentally friendly to moderately so. Those that use a high percentage of post-consumer recycled materials, agricultural by-products and nontoxic bonding agents are the best choices for the environment. In addition, high-grade composite decking can last more than fifty years with no mainte-nance. Wood decks, by comparison, have to be regularly stained and sealed. Even with diligent maintenance, a wood deck is vulnerable to weather and pests and typically has a life span of a fraction of composite decking.

Dolphin Safe Despite continuous efforts by the U.S. Commerce Department to weaken the "Dolphin Safe" label, for now it remains strong and applies only to tuna caught without chasing, encircling or intentionally setting purse seine nets on dolphins—a practice responsible for the capture, injury and death of millions of dolphins.

Electric (Vehicles) An electric car is powered by an electric motor, which in turn is powered by a controller, which is powered by a rechargeable battery pack. According to the Electric Auto Association, an electric car is 35 to 97 percent cleaner than a compa-rable gas car, including the pollution gener-ated by the electric power plant. The 35 percent number applies to states that rely heavily on "dirty" sources of power, such as coal. The 97 percent number applies to states that use a higher percentage of hydro, wind and solar to produce electricity. The

major challenges with electric vehicles today are the weight of the batteries, the long charge time and limited vehicle range per charge. The future of electric vehicles lies in fuel cell technology. See also, *Fuel Cell Powered.*

Energy Efficient An "Energy Efficient" claim implies that the product uses a reduced amount of energy in its use compared to previous or conventional use by a similar product. Energy-efficient products reduce both resource depletion and the adverse environmental impacts associated with the overuse and misuse of our energy fuels. See also, *Energy Star.*

Energy Star A program of the U.S. EPA charged with evaluating and determining energy consumed and/or saved by products that either rely on energy to run—such as appliances and home electronics—or can reduce energy use through there application, such as insulation and windows. The Energy Star label means a product meets minimum energy-efficiency standards.

According to the EPA, if every consumer, business and organization in the United States made their product choices and building improvement decisions with Energy Star, over the next decade the national annual energy bill would be reduced by about $200 billion.

Fluoride Free Fluoride is a by-product of

industry and when emitted into the environment, has considerable potential for producing ecological damage. The EPA recognizes that fluoride emissions have adverse effects on livestock and vegetation, but maintains that its effect on humans is negligible. If this sounds inconceivable to you, avoid fluoridated products.

Free Farmed This label is administered by the American Humane Association and testifies that dairy cows, chickens, cattle and hogs are raised humanely and under healthy living conditions.

Free Range, Free Roaming, Pasture Raised (beef, pork) If proposed U.S. Standards for Livestock and Meat Marketing Claims are adopted this year, these labels will apply to cattle that had continuous and unconfined access to pasture throughout their life cycle, and to swine that had continuous access to pasture for at least 80 percent of their production cycle.

Free Range (poultry) For poultry producers to legally use the "Free Range" label, the USDA requires that their animals be allowed free access to the outdoors for a "significant portion" of each day. The problem with the law is that "significant portion" is not defined. The label guarantees only that for some undefined portion of each day a door was left open, but does not guarantee animals ever made it outside. To find out if the label on your poultry products has

meaning, you'll need to call the producer and ask them for specifics on their rearing practices.

Fuel Cell Powered Fuel cells could be the zero-emissions power source that revolutionizes electric power for cars and even our homes. The fuel cell system operates by electrochemically combining hydrogen with oxygen to generate electricity. Hydrogen fuel cells produce only water vapor emissions.

Fuel Efficient One of the most important things you can do to reduce your contribution to emissions of carbon dioxide is to buy the most fuel-efficient vehicle possible that fits your needs. Fuel-efficient vehicles produce less air pollution and global warming emissions per mile driven than other vehicles.

GMO Free Genetically engineered (GE) plants, also known as genetically modified organisms (GMOs), are the product of genetic mutation. The genetic manipulation of plants involves introducing genes from essentially any organism into a plant, including inserting animal genes into a tomato, for example, so that the plant will bear unnatural but "desirable" characteristics. A number of scientists fear that GMOs could ruin ecosystems by creating super weeds, killing beneficial insects, and contaminating the food supply by cross-pollinating with natural plant species.

Grass Fed The USDA has proposed minimum requirements for the claim "Grass Fed." If adopted, "Grass Fed" will apply to an animal that receives at least 80 percent of their primary energy source from grass, green or range pasture, or forage throughout its life cycle. According to John Robbins, author of *The Food Revolution,* raising beef on pasture grass is less polluting, more energy efficient and more sustainable than raising beef on grain, but the benefits are relative. Past and present abusive grazing practices on our public lands have had devastating results. Cattle grazing in the West has polluted streams and rivers, displaced competing wildlife, and destroyed native plants and grasses on a massive scale. A number of experts consider ranching to be the rural West's most harmful influence. If you cannot give up meat, look for grass-fed animals raised humanely under sustainable standards.

Green Legally, the term "Green" is meaning-less. If a manufacturer is using the term, call them to ascertain its meaning.

Green-e A voluntary certification program that sets consumer protection and environ-mental standards for renewable electricity products, and verifies that Green-e certified products meet these standards. Under the requirements, acceptable products would get a minimum of 50 percent of the electricity supply from a list of eligible renewable resources.

Green Energy Green energy often refers to a mix of energy sources that have been combined to supply electricity that is less harmful to the environment. These sources should all be clean and renewable, but some power plants may mix clean sources with fossil fuel or nuclear sources. To make sure you are really buying green power, request a disclosure label from the supplier, which will tell you the exact mix of energy sources used and the emissions produced.

Green Seal An independent, nonprofit organization that evaluates and recommends products based on criteria that emphasize pollution prevention and environmentally responsible life cycle management. For a list of recommended products within various categories, including lawn care equipment and general purpose cleaners, visit their Web site at *greenseal.org.*

Hybrid Hybrid cars combine an electric motor with a gasoline engine to get above-average gas mileage and produce below-average emissions. A typical hybrid releases 90 percent less smog pollution and 50 percent fewer greenhouse gases compared to the cleanest conventional vehicles on the road today.

LCD Liquid Crystal Display technology is considered environmentally preferable to the CRT and plasma technologies because LCDs consume much less energy, emit no radiation and are lighter so environmental impacts from shipping are reduced.

Low Emissions Vehicle (LEV) Under the California Emission Standard, vehicles that meet strict emission levels for non-methane organic gases (NMOG), oxides of nitrogen, and carbon monoxide (CO) may qualify for one of five low-emissions categories: (1) transitional low-emission vehicles (TLEVs), (2) low-emission vehicles (LEVs), (3) ultra-low emission vehicles (ULEVs), (4) super ultra-low emission vehicle (SULEV) and (5) zero-emission vehicles (ZEVs). Under the National Low-Emission Vehicle Program, similar categories have less stringent standards.

Natural Except in meat and poultry processing, the term *natural* is meaningless in legal terms.

Natural (meat and poultry) The USDA permits any product containing no artificial ingredient or added color, and that is only minimally processed, to be labeled "Natural."

No Antibiotics Used or Raised Without Antibiotics These terms may be used on labels for meat or poultry products if sufficient documentation is provided by the producer to the USDA demonstrating that the animals were raised without antibiotics. Heavy antibiotic use on factory farms causes more strains of drug-resistant bacteria, which are transferred to humans who eat treated animals. As a result, antibiotics used to combat human diseases are becoming ineffective. Animals raised under less crowded and healthier conditions do not need excessive antibiotics to avoid disease. See *Free Farmed*.

No Hormones Administered (beef) Refers to beef livestock that have never received supplemental hormones, from birth to harvest. Animals that are administered synthetic hormones experience atypical, rapid growth. Growing scientific evidence emphasizes that exposing people to hormone residues in meat and meat products can potentially cause neurobiological (endocrine) effects, developmental effects, immunotoxicity, reproductive and immunological effects, genotoxicity and carcinogenicity.[2] Growth-promoting hormones are not only found in the tissue of treated animals, but they are also excreted into the environment. Agricultural runoff tainted with hormones ends up in water downstream of feedlots and can enter the food chain and drinking water.

No VOCs or Low VOCs Substances called volatile organic compounds (VOCs) are common in paints, paint strippers and other solvents, household cleaning products and air fresheners, floor polishes, craft supplies, fuels and automotive products, and hair-styling products. All of these products can release VOCs that contribute to the formation of ground-level ozone, or smog. There is no national standard definition for "No VOCs" or "Low VOCs," but products whose VOC concentrations are below the legal limits for their product class can claim "Low VOCs," and those which test negative for VOCs may claim "No VOCs."

Nontoxic "Toxic" means poisonous, which means harmful or deadly if exposure exceeds a certain amount. Chemicals that are Persistent, Bioaccumulative and Toxic (PBT) do not readily break down in the environment and accumulate in the tissues of animals and human beings. Their risk to humans and ecosystems is deeply concerning because, as the EPA puts it, they "transfer rather easily among air, water, and land, and span boundaries of programs, geography, and generations." The more toxins humans and wildlife are exposed to, the higher the risk of biological mutations and even death. With safer, nontoxic alternatives to toxic products relatively easy to find in the marketplace, there is no need to tolerate the presence of PBT chemicals in products we use in our everyday lives.

NutriClean Fruits and vegetables that have been found to have pesticide residues no greater than .05 ppm (part per million) may qualify.

Organic As of October 2002, the USDA became the official accreditation agency for organic products with their National Organic Program. Food and fiber grown or produced in accordance with the National Organic Standards Act are done so without toxic pesticides and fertilizers, synthetic hormones, antibiotics, sewage sludge, GMOs or irradiation. Under the National Organic Program, "100% Organic" means all product ingredients are organic, "Organic" means that 95 percent of product ingredients are organic, and "Made with Organic Ingredients" means at least 70 percent of the ingredients are organically grown. Look for the "USDA Organic" label, or the marks of those accredited by the USDA. For a list of USDA-accredited certifying agents, visit the Agricultural Marketing Service's Web site at *ams.usda.gov/nop.*

Ozone Safe or Ozone Friendly A claim of "Ozone Safe" implies that the product contains no chemicals that will deplete the upper ozone or contribute to ground ozone. The ozone layer in the upper atmosphere forms naturally and protects us from the sun's harmful ultraviolet rays. In contrast, ozone on the ground is the result of man-made emissions and is a pollutant.

Pesticide Free or No Pesticides There is no standard definition for the general claim of "Pesticide Free." A grower might use this or similar language to imply the absence of the use of any pesticides in the growing process. Another might use it to imply the absence of significant or detectable pesticide residues based on tests in the field or after

> "I know of no more encouraging fact than the unquestioned ability of a man to elevate his life by conscious endeavor." **Henry David Thoreau**

harvest. There's really no way of knowing unless you can track down the grower for comment.

Phosphate Free When phosphates, present primarily in dishwasher and laundry detergents, are introduced into waterways via storm drains, the result can be excessive algae growth. The presence of too much algae can lead to depleted oxygen levels and pollution, killing aquatic life. Some states have banned phosphates in laundry detergents and other cleaning products. If your state hasn't issued a ban, or if you're buying a product that is exempt from restrictions, look for the phosphate-free label.

rBGH Free or rBST Free (dairy) Synthetic recombinant Bovine Growth Hormone (known as rBGH, rBST and Posilac) is a genetically engineered drug that is injected into cows to artificially stimulate excessive milk production. The FDA approved the hormone in 1993, claiming milk from rBGH-treated cows was safe. The following years have seen much evidence against, and many challenges to, the safety of rBGH—both for cows and people. Canada, Australia, New Zealand, Japan and European Union nations have banned rBGH milk, yet for over a decade the U.S. FDA has refused to repeal its approval, and the use of rBGH is widespread among American dairy farmers.

Reclaimed or Recovered (general) Materials can be reclaimed already disassembled;

e.g., from salvage yards, or from anything built and then reused for new applications. Reclaimed wood from old structures is a coveted material today, and is being transformed into beautiful flooring, furniture and architectural elements for the home. And product designers' ingenuity knows no bounds when it comes to fashioning reclaimed parts from washing machines, computers and bicycles, for example, into usable consumer goods.

Reclaimed, Recovered or Salvaged (wood) There is no standard definition for the use of these terms. "Salvaged" to one producer may mean cut from standing underwater trees and to another mean removed from an abandoned building. To understand the finer points, you may need to make an inquiry.

Recyclable A recyclable material or product is one that, after its useful life, can be remanufactured into another useful material or product, thereby keeping it out of the waste stream. The Federal Trade Commission (FTC) stipulates that a package or product should not be marketed as recyclable unless it can be collected, separated or otherwise recovered from the solid waste stream for use in the manufacture or assembly of another package or product, through an established recycling program. The presence of an "established recycling program" is an important condition for the use of this claim. Several materials, though technically recyclable, are not accepted for recycling at this time. If the availability of recycling programs and collection sites are limited for a product or package, a claim of recyclability is deceptive.

Recyclable Plastic There are over 2,000 different varieties of plastic resin; as consumers, we're most familiar with types 1 through 7. The chasing arrows symbol with a number at the center was adopted by the plastics industry to identify the plastic item's primary component, or resin, not to suggest recyclability or recycled content.

Recycled According to the FTC, the recycled content claim may be made only for materials that have been recovered or otherwise diverted from the solid waste stream, either during the manufacturing process (pre-consumer) or after consumer use (post-consumer). Unless the product or package contains 100 percent recycled materials, the label must tell you how much is recycled.

Recycled Paper All recycled paper is not created equal: it can comprise as little as 10 percent recycled content, with the balance coming from virgin timber; or it can contain as much as 100 percent recycled content. Within the paper industry, if the three chasing arrows are white on a black background, it means the paper is made from 100 percent recycled content. If the arrows are black on a white background it is made up of recycled and virgin fiber and the manufacturer is required to note what

percentage comes from recycled fiber. There is also the source of recycled content to consider. Paper made with wood shavings from a lumber mill, classified as post-industrial waste, can be labeled recycled, but buying this type of paper does nothing to help support consumer recycling programs. To find paper made from recycled material collected from consumers, look for paper marked with the acronym "PCC" or "PCW," which stands for post-consumer content and post-consumer waste, respectively.

Recycled Plastic This is being used in all kinds of products including clothes, insulation, decking, furniture, carpet, trash can liners, office supplies, toys and so on.

Refurbished or Remanufactured By common definition, refurbishing means cleaning and reconditioning useable parts whereas remanufacturing goes further by introducing new parts to rebuild something (usually with mechanical or electrical parts). However, sometimes dealers use the term *refurbished* when they actually mean *remanufactured.* This is because no standard definition exists to clearly differentiate the two. When buying a refurbished or remanufactured item, ask about the process and warranty. At a minimum, make sure the unit has been carefully inspected and cleaned, that defective components have been replaced, that it has been put through rigorous testing, and that the product comes with a greater than ninety-day warranty.

Renewable Energy "Renewable" means capable of being replenished through a natural ecological process in a fairly short period of time. Renewable energy sources include solar, geothermal, wind, hydro, hydrogen and biomass.

Reusable Describes products that are built to remain useful after repeated use.

Solar Powered Solar cells, or photovoltaic (PV) cells, convert the sun's energy directly into electricity. The sun's energy is stored in a battery that runs the unit, a process that costs nothing and is nonpolluting. PV systems can contribute significantly to the mitigation of environmental impacts from conventional electricity production. While the use of PV cells does not result in pollution, there are indirect environmental impacts related to cell and module (a group of cells electrically connected) manufacturing and "end of life" waste management. To prevent or mitigate future environmental damage from the increased use of photovoltaics, the industry and the Department of Energy are proactively pursuing strategies and incentives for recycling used solar cells and manufacturing waste.

Sustainable Fishery A fishery can be a species of fish or stock of fish. A sustainable fishery is one that has not been depleted or harvested in ways that harm the ocean ecosystem. The London-based Marine Stewardship Council (MSC) provides its label to fisheries that meet strict, peer-reviewed standards of sustainability. The MSC has certified only a limited number of fisheries worldwide, and the only U.S. fishery to be certified is Alaska salmon. For more choices, Monterey Bay Aquarium has devised a SeafoodWatch wallet-size card to help consumers choose seafood that is better for the oceans. The SeafoodWatch card is viewable online at *mbayaq.org/cr/-seafoodwatch.asp* and can be downloaded and printed for reference when shopping.

Sustainable Forestry Timber operations that are certified sustainable do not take from the forest more than the forest needs to furnish the following essential protections and more: water and soil conservation, preservation of wildlife and habitat, and maintenance of forest composition and function. Different accrediting organizations have different standards, but generally, the Forest Stewardship Council (FSC) certification is trusted by environmentalists. Look for the FSC mark of certification when buying virgin wood products, or the marks of certifying agents accredited by FSC. For a list of FSC-approved certifiers, visit *fscus.org.*

Transitional Products of farms labeled "Transitional" or "Certified Transitional" are transitioning to organic certification. The label can only be used following at least one full year of production using organic methods that comply with the National

Organic Standards Act and its regulations. The entire transitional process takes three years.

Tree Free (paper) Tree-free paper can be made from plants like kenaf, hemp, bamboo, cotton, and flax or from agricultural by-products such as banana stalks, sugarcane, coffee skins, cornstalks, wheat straw and tobacco fiber.

Unbleached/Non-chlorine Bleached See *Chlorine Free.*

Used The most earth-wise purchase may be that of a used item, since it obviates overproduction of new items and the disposal of useful ones. Except in cases where the continued use of an old item, such as an inefficient freezer circa 1970, would contribute greater harm to the environment than replacing it with a newer, more energy-efficient model, buying a secondhand item is environmentally preferable to buying new.

Wildcrafted or Wildharvested
Wildharvesting is the sustainable harvesting of wild plants in their natural setting. Careful attention is paid to the sustainable yield of the land so that the same botanical resources can be wildharvested year after year. A "Wildcrafted" or "Wildharvested" claim is sometimes made without verification. There are, however, several competing certification agencies with varying standards

and levels of oversight. SmartWood and the Soil Association, both FSC-accredited certifiers, have incorporated detailed performance expectations and thresholds for best management practices of Non-Timber Forest Products (NTFPs), and the Canadian Ethical Wildcrafting Association (CEWA) certifies ethical wildcrafters with its own set of standards and guidelines.

THE COST OF GREEN

It cannot be said, categorically, that earth-friendlier products cost more than their conventional counterparts. They can cost more, but just as often they cost less, as when they rely on recycled and/or recovered inputs and reduce waste expenditures and liability for the manufacturer. For some things you will pay a little more, for others a little less, but in the end, a well-rounded green-buying strategy can save you money overall in the following ways:

- Buying less reduces spending.
- Purchasing staples in bulk costs less per pound than smaller-packaged portions.
- Used items cost a fraction of what new items cost.
- Quality products will last, so you can avoid repair and replacement costs.
- Borrowing and renting seldom-used, costly equipment obviates large purchases.
- Energy- and fuel-efficient consumer products save on energy costs.

- Using safe, nontoxic products means fewer health-care expenditures resulting from exposure to skin, eye and respiratory irritants.
- Concentrated products can cost less per use.
- Qualifying electric and clean-fuel vehicles (including hybrids), and energy-efficient appliances and products are eligible for federal income tax deductions.

Buying earth-friendly products will also help bolster demand. As demand for these products increases, so will supply—driving prices down. Adopting more conservative and earth-wise buying habits is a legitimate and sensible long-term approach to personal savings.

CHAPTER 5:
GREEN SHOPPING ONLINE

The expectation of great selection, convenience and saving time has inspired many to venture into online stores. Busy people who can't seem to make it to a store during its normal business hours can be greatly served by electronic commerce. For the earth-conscious online shopper, there's more good news: new research suggests that shopping online has environmental benefits too. According to the Center for Energy and Climate Solutions, we can save energy and protect land by shopping online. The transportation energy used to ship items from a warehouse to homes is less than the combined energy used to ship to retailers and to get around town in our cars. Internet shopping also reduces land development for retail stores and parking lots.

The busy person may only have their coffee break or a narrow window between putting the kids down and collapsing from exhaustion to shop online, so finding products and checking out has to be quick and efficient. The Web businesses identified in this chapter not only offer earth-friendly products, but they also provide well-organized sites that make online shopping as simple and straightforward as possible—the busy person browsing or shopping online requires nothing less.

This chapter includes just some of the innovative green businesses that have opened stores in cyberspace. The vast majority of these companies offer online sales; a few are informational sites that provide other means for learning more about or purchasing their products. There are many, many more good green businesses on the Web; they simply could not all fit on these pages.

Supports REUSE!

PeeWee CLOTHING Exchange

Supports SUSTAINABLE AGRICULTURE

Organic BABY FOOD Co

HEMP Luggage Company

Supports INDUSTRIAL HEMP

BABY AND MOTHER

Alternative Baby (*alternativebaby.com*)
Baby Bunz & Co. (*babybunz.com*)
Baby's Enchanted Garden (*babysenchantedgarden.com*)
Birdie's Room (*birdiesroom.com*)
EcoBaby (*ecobaby.com*)

BATH TIME

Babecology (*babecology.com*) Formulated with natural plant and fruit extracts.
Erbaviva (*erbaviva.com*) Unique products to nurture and protect baby's delicate skin.
Trusted Care (*trustedcare.com*)
Everything for during and after bath time.

DIAPERING

Punkin-Butt (*punkinbutt.com*) A wide selection of cloth diapers and a few other things too.
Fuzbaby (*fuzbaby.com*) Diapers plus information on the eco-friendliness and absorbency of cloth-diaper fibers.

FOOD

Baby Organic (*babyorganic.com*) Dairy or soy-based organic formula.
Earth's Best (*earthsbest.com*) A variety of organic products.

FOR MOMS

Earth Mama, Angel Baby (*earthmamaangelbaby.com*) Natural products and information for pregnancy, labor, postpartum, breast-feeding and babies.

> "There is enough on earth for everybody's need, but not for everyone's greed."
> **Mahatma Gandhi**

Motherlove (*motherlove.com*) Herbal products for pregnancy, birth and breastfeeding.

BATH AND BODY
Aromaleigh (*aromaleigh.com*) Mineral cosmetics and natural skin care.
Aubrey Organics (*aubrey-organics.com*) Hair and skin-care products.
Avalon Natural Products (*avalonnaturalproducts.com*) Facial, body, lip and hair care.
Aveda (*aveda.com*) Makeup, Pure-Fume, hair and skin care, and bath accessories.
Azida, Inc. (*azida.com*) Personal care products featuring blended hemp oil and ground hemp meal with other natural ingredients.
Honeybee Gardens (*honeybeegardens.com*) Products for men and women.
The Organic Makeup Company (*theorganicmakeupcompany.com*) Pure, natural cosmetics made in Canada.
Raining Rose (*rainingrose.com*) Plant-based oils and aromatherapy-grade essential oils go into lip balm, soap, skin-care and hair-care products.
Terressentials (*terressentials.com*) Handcrafted natural and organic personal-care products with no synthetic petrochemical or oleochemical ingredients of any kind.

MAKE-IT-YOURSELF SUPPLIES
Cranberry Lane (*cranberrylane.com*) Kits for making your own natural body-care products.
Mountain Rose Herbs

(*mountainroseherbs.com*) Bulk beauty product ingredients.

CLEANING
Country Save (*countrysave.com*) Products for the laundry, kitchen and general-purpose cleaning.
Mountain Green (*mtngreen.com*) All-natural cleaning products: no petroleum-based cleaning agents or harsh conventional chemicals.
Seventh Generation (*seventhgeneration.com*) Complete line of nontoxic household products.
Soapworks (*soapworks.com*) Nontoxic and biodegradable. Made of all-natural vegetable ingredients.

CLOTHING AND ACCESSORIES
FASHION
Coolnotcruel (*coolnotcruel.com*) Urban chic fashion made of environmentally responsible materials.
Earth Speaks (*earthspeaks.com*) Organically made, beautiful women's fashions.
The Green Loop (*thegreenloop.com*) Style and sustainability in fashion and basics for men, women and children.
Hempy's (*hempys.com*) Hip clothes and accessories made from hemp, organic cotton and recycled synthetics.
Sahara Organics (*saharaorganics.com*) Organic cotton-, hemp- and silk-blended apparel.
Under the Canopy (*underthecanopy.com*) Their EcoFashion line is made from natural and organic fibers.

CASUAL AND ACTIVEWEAR

Blue Canoe Bodywear (*bluecanoe.com*) Organic body wear and PVC-free yoga mats.

Earth Creations (*earthcreations.net*) Clay-dyed hemp, organic cotton and linen casual wear.

Of the Earth (*oftheearth.com*) Natural-fiber apparel for your active or casual lifestyle.

Prana (*prana.com*) Hemp, organic cotton and recycled silk are woven into casual apparel and workout gear.

SWEATERS AND OUTERWEAR

French Creek Sheep and Wool Company (*frenchcreeksw.com*) Meticulously made shearlings, sweaters and garments of natural fiber.

Indigenous Designs (*indigenousdesigns.com*) Eco-sensitive clothing made from natural fibers such as merino wool, alpaca and organic cotton.

Patagonia (*patagonia.com*) All-cotton sportswear is 100 percent organic. Other ecological fabrics include hemp and recycled polyester.

FOOTWEAR

Alternative Outfitters (*alternativeoutfitters.com*) Stylish, fun and hip cruelty-free shoes and handbags.

Ecosandals (*ecosandals.com*) Sandals made in part from 100 percent recycled tire tread rubber and enhanced with leather or denim, beadwork and artistic detail.

Shoes With Souls (*shoeswithsouls.com*) Makes Deja and Daya brand footwear—100 percent vegan.

Simple Shoes (*simpleshoes.com*) Look for their Green Toe brand of shoes made with low-impact materials.

ACCESSORIES

Artisan Gear (*artisangear.com*) Casual, durable hemp canvas bags for travel and adventure.

Maggie's Organics (*organicclothes.com*) Socks, camisoles, aprons, hair scrunchies, garden gloves, bags, etc.

Watership Trading Company (*watershiptrading.com*) High-quality hats using many ecological fibers.

BABIES AND TODDLERS

Bossy Baby (*bossybaby.com*) Organic, hemp and recycled-fiber clothing.

Garden Kids Clothing (*gardenkidsclothing.com*) Colorful, organic cotton clothing decorated with garden-themed patches.

Green Babies (*greenbabies.com*) Features prints with themes borrowed from nature.

Kidlets Clothing (*kidletsclothing.com*) Infant wear, children's clothing, accessories, outerwear.

Lapsaky Organic Cotton Baby Clothes (*lapsaky.com*) Great selection, style and detail from this 100 percent organic collection.

See also, *Baby & Mother*.

SPECIAL OCCASION

Conscious Clothing (*getconscious.com*) Hemp-blend wedding gowns and bridesmaids' dresses.

Organic Weddings (*organicweddings.com*) Wedding gowns made from all-natural fabrics.

Used Wedding Dress (*usedweddingdresses.com*) Gently worn wedding dresses.

A Vintage Wedding (*avintagewedding.com*) Vintage wedding gowns and dresses.

Vintage Wedding (*vintagewedding.com*) Vintage attire for the bride and groom.

Vintageous (*vintageous.com*) Vintage formal and cocktail dresses.

UNDERGARMENTS

3 Tree Apparel (*3tree.org*) Pure organic cotton underwear and undershirts for women.

Alternative Undies/Sahara Organics (*saharaorganics.com*) Undergarments for men and women.

Nordic Natural Woollens (*nordicwoollens.com*) Untreated merino wool underwear.

Osaj (*osaj.com*) Unbleached organic cotton underwear for men and women.

COMMUNICATIONS
INTERNET

SolarHost (*solarhost.com*) Web hosting and services powered by renewable energy.

EcoISP (*ecoisp.com*) Donates 50 percent of subscription fees to environmental groups.

Elfon (*elfon.com*) 100 percent wind-powered Web hosting.

Locomotive Media (*locomotivemedia.com*) Web hosting powered by wind.

LONG DISTANCE

Earth Tones (*earthtones.com*) Gives 100 percent of its profits to environmental groups.

DEPARTMENT STORES

IIKH (*2kh.com*) Products with a stylish flare.

Craig's List (*craigslist.org*) An expanding resource for locating used stuff in many cities across the country.

E-Bay (*ebay.com*) To keep shopping eco-friendly, use the advanced search to find things that are used and, if possible, local.

EcoChoices (*ecochoices.com*) A hub for more than ten Web sites with one shopping cart.

Ecolution (*ecolution.com*) Clothing, footwear, bags and products for the home.

Gaiam (*gaiam.com*) Innovative, healthful products for the home and self.

GrassRoots Natural Goods (*grassrootsnaturalgoods.com*) Hemp goods for yourself, your home and your pet.

Green Home (*greenhome.com*) An environmental superstore with everything from apparel to yard and garden products.

HealthyHome.com, Inc. (*healthyhome.com*) Products and information for creating a healthy and sustainable home.

Hemp Fair (*hempfair.com*) Hemp-based products in several categories.

Rawganique (*rawganique.com*) Clothes for men, women and kids plus towels, sheets, footwear and bags.
Real Goods (*realgoods.com*) Products for inside and outside the home.
Vivavi (*vivavi.com*) Stylish, environmentally friendly products that fit modern lifestyles.

ENERGY AND APPLIANCES
CONSERVATION
AM Conservation Group, Inc. (*amconservationgroup.com*) Weatherization, water and energy-saving products and kits.
Conserv-A-Store (*conservastore.com*) Products that reduce the use of resources and energies for home and business.
Energy Federation Incorporated (*efi.org*) Products that can offer economic and environmental benefits through conservation.
The Laundry Alternative, Inc. (*laundry-alternative.com*) Compact, portable, water-efficient pressure-washing machine.
Niagara Conservation (*niagaraconservation.com*) Water and energy conservation products.

RENEWABLE ENERGY
Alternative Energy Store (*altenergystore.com*) A variety of alternative energy solutions and appliances.
Bergey WindPower (*bergey.com*) Small wind turbines for homes and businesses.
Utility Free Alternative Energy Options (*utilityfree.com*) Products for utility-free power requirements.

Solardyne Corp. (*solardyne.com*) Renewable energy equipment and high-efficiency home appliances.
Sundance Solar (*sundancesolar.com*) Solar power solutions for small portable electronics as well as panels, components and systems for bigger jobs.

ELECTRIC UTILITIES
Green-e (*green-e.org*) Switch to a cleaner, renewable electricity provider where available, or purchase Tradable Renewable Certificates to offset your home energy usage with 100 percent renewable energy.

WOOD BURNING
EcoFire Super-Grate (*ecofire.com*) Reduces pollution and increases heat from wood burning.
Summit Views Goodwood Firelogs (*summitviews.com/firelogs.html*) One hundred percent renewable, compressed logs for cleaner-burning fires.

TRANSPORTATION
Electrik Motion (*electrikmotion.com*) A wide selection of electric bikes and scooters.
ZAP! (*zapworld.com*) Personal electric transportation options.
eGO (*egovehicles.com*) Electric moped.

GAMES AND TOYS

Ampersand Press (*ampersandpress.com*) Educational and fun games that explore science, nature and the environment.

Island Treasure Toys (*islandtreasuretoys.com*) Waldorf-inspired toys made of natural materials.

Natural Play (*naturalplay.com*) Toys that encourage imaginative play and interaction with nature and the world.

North Star Toys (*waldorfresources.net/nstoys*) Nontoxic wooden puzzles and toys.

The Play Store (*playstoretoys.com*) Toys of value and quality that are better for the environment.

Rosie Hippo's Toys (*rosiehippo.com*) Many natural toys that are easy on the environment and encourage creative exploration.

GIFTS

3r Living (*3rliving.com*) Home accessories, kits for kids and healthy cleaning supplies.

Eco-Artware (*eco-artware.com*) Gifts from recycled, reused and natural materials.

Fresh Unlimited (*freshunlimited.com*) Themed gift sets considerate of the environment and the well-being of artisans and growers.

Granola Groovy (*granolagroovy.com*) Ecological, organic and fairly traded products.

Littlearth (*littlearth.com*) Reclaimed materials turned into belts, handbags, photo and CD holders, key chains, etc.

Nahempco (*nahempco.com*) Hemp-based skin care, paper, candles, bags, etc.

Organic Gift Shop (*organicgiftshop.com*) Earth-friendly gifts for babies, kids and grown-ups.

Recycled Planet Store (*recycledplanet-store.com*) Unique, colorful and functional gift line made from recycled materials.

Resource Revival (*resourcerevival.com*) Frames, clocks, sculptural storage, candlesticks and home furnishings made from recovered materials.

Rivanna Natural Designs (*rivannadesigns.com*) Handcrafted gifts and awards from natural and recycled materials.

Uhma Nagri (*uhmanagri.com*) Unique and elegant gift sets with natural wellness and fair trade themes.

WORLD GOODS

Antiki Trading Co. (*antiki.com*) Handcrafted cultural arts, home decor and gifts made by artisans using traditional materials and crafting techniques.

Global Exchange (*store.gxonlinestore.org*) Fairly traded, low-impact products from around the world.

FLOWERS

Organic Bouquet (*organicbouquet.com*) National distributor of certified organic roses and tulips.

SPECIALITY FOOD AND BEVERAGES

AllTea.com (*alltea.com*) Build your own gift basket with the teas, accessories and treats of your choice.

Allison's Gourmet Cookies (*allisons-gourmet.com*) Baked goods made with organic and animal-free ingredients.

Endangered Species Chocolate Company (*chocolatebar.com*) Organic and GMO-free Belgian chocolate bars.

Fiddler's Green Farm (*fiddlersgreenfarm.com*) Baking mixes, syrups and jams from Maine.

Grounds for Change (*groundsforchange.com*) Give the gift of a different fair-trade organic coffee of the month for three, six or twelve months.

The Organic Wine Press (*organicwine-press.com*) "Wino of the Month Club" allows you to sign up a friend to receive a different selection of organic wines for a predetermined number of months.

Pura Vida (*puravidacoffee.com*) Certified fair-trade, organic, shade-grown coffee.

Thanksgiving Coffee (*thanksgivingcoffee.com*) Pleasing gift baskets by a company that is working to transform the coffee business.

Village Organics (*villageorganics.com*) Gift baskets, boxes and specialty items.

TO THE EARTH

Alternative Gifts International (*altgifts.org*) Support for environmental or humanitarian projects can be your gift to someone for any occasion.

Just Give (*justgive.org*) Donations to your charity of choice can be made as a gift in someone else's name.

TreeGivers (*treegivers.com*) Gift tree planted in the state or listed country of your choice.

HEALTH AND HYGIENE

(Herbal supplements and remedies can be potent, even dangerous. Use caution and seek the advice of a medical professional before using botanical products.)

MotherNature.com (*mothernature.com*) Natural and organic products including vitamins and supplements, herbs, diet aids, essential oils and more, for health and wellness.

Organic Health and Beauty (*organichealthandbeauty.com*) Health products made with organic whole foods and herbs.

Terra Firma Botanicals (*terrafirmabotani-cals.com*) Herbal tinctures, salves and infused flower oils using Certified Organically Grown, Respectfully Wildcrafted herbs.

Tom's of Maine (*toms-of-maine.com*) Toothpaste, deodorant, soap, cough remedies, etc.

Whole Life Essentials (*wholelifeessentials.com*) Many products for self, health and wellness, using the finest-quality essential oils.

HERBS

Living Earth Herbs (*livingearthherbs.com*) Ethically grown and harvested herbs.

Mountain Rose Herbs (*mountainroseherbs.com*) Bulk herbs, essential oils and other bulk ingredients for those making their own products.

> "There is a difference between saying that change is hard to achieve and saying that the average person will never do anything. One is a challenge, and the other is cause for despair." **Unknown**

WOMEN'S PRODUCTS

Gladrags (*gladrags.com*) Alternative menstrual products.

The Keeper (*mykeepercup.com*) Natural rubber menstrual cup.

Lunapads (*lunapads.com*) Unique products for menstruation.

NaturalFemPro.com (*naturalfempro.com*) Organic cotton tampons.

Organic Essentials (*organicessentials.com*) Organic cotton products.

HOBBIES AND CRAFTS
TEXTILES

American Hemp (*americanhemptwine.com*) Hemp twine, cordage, yarn, rope, etc.

EnviroTextile, LLC (*envirotextile.com*) Hemp and hemp-blend textiles and yarns.

Indika (*indikahome.com*) Upholstery fabrics.

NearSea Naturals (*nearseanaturals.com*) Fabrics and notions to make your sewing projects sustainable.

KITS AND SUPPLIES

Arnold Grummer's, Inc. (*arnoldgrummer.com*) Papermaking kit and supplies.

Hemp Basics (*hempsupply.com*) Kits for rug and jewelry making.

Seven Bridges Cooperative (*breworganic.com)* Organic home-brew supplies.

Way Out Wax (*wayoutwax.com*) Candle supplies.

HOME FURNISHINGS AND DECOR
BED AND BATH

Coyuchi (*coyuchiorganic.com*) Bedding and bath products made from certified organically grown cotton or wool.

Indika (*indikahome.com*) Luxurious sheets, towels and more.

Organic Cotton Alternatives (*organiccottonalts.com*) Beds, nursery items, pillows, yoga pads, linens, pet beds, etc.

Organic Mattress (*organicmattresses.com*) Chemical-free organic beds and bedding.

Pure-Rest (*purerest.com*) Organic and natural products for your home.

White Lotus Futon (*whitelotus.net*) Futons, pillows, duvets, sheets and more.

FURNITURE

Alan Vogel Furniture (*alanvogelfurniture.com*) Custom dining tables made from reclaimed fir or pine.

Conklin's Unique Country (*uniquecountry.com*) Custom furniture crafted from antique barn wood.

Green Culture (*eco-furniture.com*) Earth-friendly furniture for every room in the house and the backyard too.

Furnature (*furnature.com*) Furniture, mattresses and bedding made without chemicals, dyes, polymers or toxins.

Pacific Rim Woodworking (*pacificrimwoodworking.com*) Maple furniture constructed with wood from managed forests in the Pacific Northwest.

Quality-Teak.com (*quality-teak.com*)
Reclaimed teak is handcrafted by artisans into quality, environmentally friendly furniture.
Tamalpais NatureWorks (*tamalpais.com*)
Furniture and furniture kits designed and constructed from natural materials.
The Wooden Duck (*thewoodenduck.com*)
Recycled wood furniture and restored antiques.
Whit McLeod (*whitmcleod.com*) Arts and Crafts furniture from reclaimed and salvaged materials.

RUGS

Fibreworks (*fibreworks.com*) Natural fiber area rugs in a variety of patterns, colors and styles.
Marge's Braided Rugs (*margesbraidedrugs.com*) Custom-made 100 percent wool braided rugs.
Natural Area Rugs (*naturalarearugs.com*)
Choose from sisal, bamboo, wool shag, etc.
NatureRugs.com (*naturerugs.com*) High-quality hand-knotted oriental rugs of 100 percent natural fibers.
Sisal Rugs Direct (*sisalrugs.com*) Sisal, wool, sea grass and mountain grass rugs.

CANDLES

Bluecorn Naturals (*beeswaxcandles.com*)
Raw natural beeswax and soy wax candles.
Britelites (*britelites.com*) Soy candles offering a nontoxic, biodegradable, soot-free and longer-burning alternative to paraffin candles.

TABLEWARE

Bambu (*bambuhome.com*) Serving ware, bowls, plates, baskets and cutting boards made from renewable bamboo.
Fire and Light (*fireandlight.com*)
Dinnerware made from crushed recycled glass in a rich spectrum of colors and textures.
Green Glass, Inc. (*greenglass.com*) Stylish, unique goblets and tumblers.
Natural Spaces (*naturalspaces.com*)
Colorful, recycled-glass dinnerware.
Recycled Glassworks (*recycledglassworks.com*) Unique handmade dishes, platters and bowls made from recycled window-type glass.

WINDOW TREATMENTS

Earthshade.com (*earthshade.com*) Natural window fashions.

HOME IMPROVEMENT

(See also Building and Home Improvement in chapter 7 for recommended supplier databases.)

ENVIRONMENT FRIENDLY HOME CENTERS

EcoProducts (*ecoproducts.com*) Business, household and building products.
Environmental Home Center (*environmentalhomecenter.com*)
Green Building Supply (*greenbuildingsupply.com*)

INDOOR PEST CONTROL

PetChaser (*sonictechnology.com*)
Repels rodents with high-frequency ultrasound waves.

White Mountain Natural Products, Inc.
(*whitemountainnatural.com*) Makers of
Di-Atomate, diatomaceous earth for safely
killing many insects.
The Mouse Depot (*themousedepot.com*)
Catch-and-release mousetrap.

OFFICE AND SCHOOL SUPPLIES
Dolphin Blue (*dolphinblue.com*)
Environmentally responsible office supplies.
Green Earth Office Supply
(*greenearthofficesupply.com*) Products for
the office and classroom.

INKJET AND LASER CARTRIDGES
Discount Toners (*discountoners.com*)
Universal Toner Refill Kit for empty laser
cartridges and remanufactured cartridges.
Hampton Toner & Ink
(*hamptontonerandink.com*) Empties are
cleaned, refilled, tested and returned.
Inkjet Domain (*inkjetdomain.com*)
Recycles empty inkjet cartridges.
Inkliquidator (*store.inkliquidator.net*)
Cartridges and refill kits.
Model Inkjet (*modelinkjet.com*)
Send empties to be professionally remanu-
factured, tested and returned to you within
five to seven days.
CBD Toner Recharge (*recharge.net*)
Toner and ink cartridges.

USED AND REFURBISHED COMPUTERS
Laptop Kings (*laptopkings.com*)
Skyex Laptop Store (*skyexlaptopstore.com*)

OFFICE FURNITURE
AlterEco Furniture (*bamboocabinets.com*)
Cabinets, desks, and work stations featuring
bamboo and sustainable and salvage wood.
Baltix Furniture (*baltix.com*) Workstations
and home office furniture made from
sustainable and recycled materials.
Dauphin (*dauphin.com*) Environmentally
sensitive, ergonomic office seating.
Planet Squared
(*planetsquared.com/products.htm*) Modular
furniture arrangements produced from
nontoxic, recycled materials.
Studio eg (*studioeg.com*) Aesthetic and
functional office furniture made from
recycled, reused and nontoxic materials.

OUTDOORS/LAWN AND GARDEN PROTECTION
All Terrain (*www.allterrainco.com*) Insect
repellent, sun protection and rubs.
Bug Baffler (*bugbaffler.com*) Insect-barrier
clothing.
See also, Bath and Body.

LAWN AND GARDEN
Clean Air Gardening Company
(*cleanairgardening.com*) Manual and
electric lawn and garden equipment, rain
barrels and more.
Composters.com (*composters.com*)
Large selection of composting bins and
tumblers, rain barrels and more.

Extremely Green Gardening Company
(*extremelygreen.com*) Proven organic products and practices.

The Natural Gardening Company
(*naturalgardening.com*) Complete organic gardening source.

Natural Insect Control
(*natural-insect-control.com*) Beneficial insects, traps, lures, barriers and controls.

Peaceful Valley Farm Supply
(*groworganic.com*) Tools and supplies for organic gardeners and farmers.

Planet Natural (*planetnatural.com*) Garden and home supplies.

Seeds of Change (*seedsofchange.com*) One hundred percent organic seeds.

Seeds Trust (*seedstrust.com*) Vegetable, wildflower, native grass and herb seeds.

Urban Garden Center
(*urbangardencenter.com*) Compost bins, rain barrels and recycled furniture.

FURNITURE AND ACCESSORIES

American Recycled Plastic, Inc. (*itsrecycled.com*) Adirondacks, benches, rockers, side tables, fencing, decking, planters and landscape ties.

Bamboo Fencer (*bamboofencer.com*) Bamboo products for the yard and garden including rolled fencing, trellises, edging and poles.

MetaMorf Design (*metamorfdesign.com*) Benches, beach chairs and side tables in bright colors.

PAPER PRODUCTS
GIFT WRAP AND GREETING CARDS
Buy Gift Wrap
(*buygiftpaper.com/Recycled.htm*) This no-frills site offers many colors in recycled gift wrap.

Doodle Greetings (*doodlegreetings.com*) Greeting cards using the most environmentally responsible papers.

Good Cause Greeting
(*goodcausegreetings.com*) Recycled cards. A portion of the sales benefit the charity profiled on the back of the cards.

Goodgeweb (*goodge.com*) Fine greeting cards using high-quality recycled papers and soy-based inks.

Recycle Paper Greetings
(*recycledpapergreetings.com*) Humorous and creative cards printed on 100 percent recycled stock.

St. Jude's Ranch
(*stjudesranch.org/content/cardprogram.asp*) Cards that have lovingly been made using old card fronts.

INVITATIONS AND ANNOUNCEMENTS
Of the Earth (*custompaper.com*) Custom-made invitations infused with your choice of ingredients.

Twisted Limb Paperworks
(*twistedlimbpaper.com*) Recycled, handmade paper stitched into distinctive invitations and announcements.

SPECIALTY AND BOUND PAPER

Acorn Designs (*acorndesigns.org*) Journals, note cards, notepads and stationery.

Costa Rica Natural (*ecopaper.com*) Agendas, notebooks, desktop publishing items, and stationery featuring banana, coffee and cigar papers.

Green Field Paper Co. (*greenfieldpaper.com*) Paper products made from hemp, organic cotton and recycled junk mail, among other things.

New England Cartographics, Inc. (*necartographics.com*) Stationery recycled from outdated government surplus topographic maps.

Nomad Adventure Journals (*nomadjournals.com*) Journals to record your adventures. Produced with recycled paper and printed with soy-based inks.

Wildlight Press, Inc. (*grizzlyden.com*) Nature-wildlife photo calendars, organizers and diaries. All printed on environmental papers.

OFFICE AND CLASSROOM PAPERS

GreenLine Paper Co. (*greenlinepaper.com*) Many papers and paper products for work and school.

House of Doolittle (*houseofdoolittle.com*) Desk calendars and appointment books. *See also, Office and School Supplies.*

PERSONAL CHECKS

The Check Gallery (*checkgallery.com*) Environmentally friendly checks.

Message Products (*messageproducts.com*) Personal checks, bank checks and check products utilizing recycled fibers, soy and hemp.

PET PRODUCTS
NATURAL PET MARKET

(*naturalpetmarket.com*) Food, gift ideas, toys, remedies and supplements.

Naturespet.com (*naturespet.com*) Natural and holistic products from food to grooming products.

Only Natural Pet Store (*onlynaturalpet.com*) Natural and holistic pet products for dogs and cats.

Planet Dog (*planetdog.com*) Gear for dogs. Beds, backpacks, leashes, toys, etc. Many products are made from recycled materials or natural fibers.

Spectrum (*epetfood.com*) Certified organic pet foods, animal health and pet-care products.

Your Parrot Place (*yourparrotplace.com*) Parrot food, toys and supplies.

GROOMING AND HEALTH

CyberCanine.com (*cybercanine.com*) Botanical dog-grooming products.

Organipetz (*organipetz.com*) Shampoo bars made with essential oils and herbs.

FOOD

Eagle Pack (*eaglepack.com*) Holistic, natural pet food.

The Honest Kitchen
(*thehonestkitchen.com*) Wholesome ingredients that have been gently dehydrated and form the base for a raw or other home-made diet.

Natural Balance, Inc.
(*naturalbalanceinc.com*) Natural pet foods including organic varieties.

The Original Dog Biscuit (*originaldogbiscuit.com*) Dog treats in many flavors made with mostly organic ingredients.

Chewtastics
(*eisenman.com/web-sites/chewtastics*) All-natural beef dog chews.

Tail Wagging Bakery
(*tailwaggingbakery.com*) Certified organic dog and cat treats.

PROBLEM SOLVING

Composters.com (*composters.com*) In-ground pet waste composters and biodegradable, compostable clean-up bags.

Earth's Balance/Millennium Lawns, Inc.
(*earthsbalance.com*) Natural solutions for pet problems around the home, like dog urine burns in lawns and offensive cat litter box odors.

Oops... I Pooped (*oopsipooped.net*) Biodegradable bags for cleaning up pet waste.

REUSABLE BAGS

EchoBag (*echobag.com*) Fabric gift bags you can use again and again.

EcoBags (*ecobags.com*) Natural and organic cotton totes, produce bags, lunch bags, etc.

Lagniappe Gift Wrap
(*lagniappegiftwrap.com*) Natural and recycled-fiber reusable gift bags.

Reusablebags.com (*reusablebags.com*) All kinds of bags for different uses.

Wrapsacks.com (*wrapsacks.com*) Cloth gift bags in colorful, hand-dyed batik designs.

CHAPTER 6:
GETTING INVOLVED

Aside from individual actions, to meaningfully preserve and protect the environment, we need active involvement and cooperation from world nations and multinational corporations as well. Governing organizations must take a major role in shaping, mandating and enforcing policies that will control pollution and manage dwindling and stressed natural resources. And corporations need to demonstrate accountability for the impacts of their commercial and industrial activities. Unfortunately, too many of those with authority and responsibility for stemming environmental damage and resource deficits are making a mess of things. We therefore have two choices: we can either let decision-makers know that we care, are paying attention and won't stand by while consequential acts against the environment are committed, or we can remain silent— leaving them to the influences of the moneyed, vocal minority and those with agendas devoid of ecologically sound principles.

A quiet citizenry means lobbyists and campaign contributors are tipping the scale in favor of policies that benefit industry and special interest groups at the expense of sensible environmental protection. And without notable consumer input, corporate policies are not predicated on green ethics or public opinion. Instead of being frustrated and angry by the lack of environmental caretaking, you can do something about it. You can use the Internet to advocate better policies that defend the planet. A number of environmental and watchdog groups have Web sites that help the public stay informed and take action; and Internet technology has made taking action easier than ever—raising public input to a whole new level.

> "Government is too big and too important to be left to the politicians."
> **Chester Bowles**

TAKING BACK CONTROL

People want a clean environment; this has been well established through national surveys and polls by such organizations as Gallup. At the same time, some powerful industries and special interests are fighting for fewer and weaker environmental laws. In order to be heard above the drone of lobbyists that have become a formidable fixture in American politics, the public must strive to replace them as the proverbial squeaky wheel. Speak out: if concerned citizens want to undermine private agendas that cause long-term or irreversible damage to the environment and lead to taxpayer liabilities, they must communicate with the men and women who are writing and passing the laws. The integrity of our environmental laws, and their enforcement, will mean the difference between safeguarding the wellness of the planet or allowing for its affliction and degeneration.

It's not just the government that needs to hear from the public. Corporations operating with disregard for public health and the environment can devastate national environmental goals. Therefore, the public must also challenge our corporate "citizens" to operate legally and ethically—and hold them accountable for anything less. As consumers, we are particularly powerful to influence corporate behavior. Simply knowing a disreputable company's products and boycotting them en masse can cause a company to change coarse.

More Americans must get involved on this level. Whether that means sending a letter to a cabinet secretary or boycotting a company's products, finding out about and seizing opportunities for action has never been easier.

TAKING ACTION MADE EASY

Taking action doesn't have to include picketing city hall or giving hours of your time to a nonprofit organization. Taking action by means of occasional phone calls, letters or faxes to lawmakers and decision-makers is now feasible even for the busy person. This formerly intimidating endeavor has, with the advent of the Internet, become undeniably easy. The Internet has empowered the masses to engage in a simple and convenient form of activism called *electronic activism*. Anyone with access to a computer and the Internet can find out about pending environmental policy decisions and environmental malfeasance that demand our attention, and take action to influence an outcome or solution.

News of corporate improprieties or pending environmental policy decisions on which public comment is needed is commonly called an *action alert*. Web sites providing tools and resources for taking action regularly post action alerts for their visitors and e-mail subscribers. The action alert first signals the reader to an opportunity or to a problem and a solution, then calls upon the reader to take action. Taking action can be as simple as typing your name into a form so that it can be added to the signature line of a prewritten letter. In this case, providing a prewritten letter saves busy people the time and effort of researching and composing their own letters, thus greatly increasing public response to the action alert. Other forms of electronic activism include signing online petitions, printing sample letters for faxing, or writing your own letter or making phone calls with the help of provided talking points.

MAKING IT COUNT

Electronic activism isn't perfect: it is being employed with more and more frequency, and the Capitol, some claim, has been besieged by e-mail. E-mail campaigns may produce hundreds of thousands of letters that look and read alike. Some critics of electronic activism believe that the homogeneous mail it produces gives the appearance of detached, dispassionate support, and thus is not as effective as personal letters, phone calls and face-to-face visits. And in 2003, a single federal agency (U.S. Forest Service [USFS]) went so far as to announce they would disregard form mail, arguing that identical e-mails, postcards, etc., that say the same thing tell them nothing—nonsense.[1] E-mails that say the same thing attest that multiple individuals are in precise agreement. And writing notes by hand and participating in face-to-face meetings may be more intimate and outstanding, but to hold the busy person to this standard is to silence them. Whether putting pen to paper to write original comments or signing a form letter, both are an expression of interest and concern on the part of the sender, and it does not discount the sincerity of the message. So, if it comes down to either sending a quick e-mail or not, *send the e-mail.* It's better to hitch on to an e-mail campaign via the Internet than to do nothing at all.

All of the above being true, if you *have* the time, *take* the time to personalize e-letters. Even though prepared letters are meant to facilitate and quicken your response to action alerts, your understanding of the issue at hand and your support for the solution should be genuine and informed. And if this is the case, you should have no problem spending one or two additional minutes online to personalize the sample letters that are provided.

Personalizing a campaign form letter doesn't have to be time-consuming or difficult, and it will set your letter apart from others. Write a sentence or two explaining why you personally care enough to send the letter. Prove to the recipient that you have individual and cogent opinions of your own, and express those opinions right off the bat within the first paragraph, if appropriate.

"All that is needed for the forces of evil to triumph is for good men to do nothing." **Edmund Burke**

Also, delete some of the wordiness—even some of the arguments the letter makes—to differentiate the look, length and content of your letter. The aggregate of all the letters sent will cover the substantive points the campaign is making, so emphasizing only those that are particularly important to you will suffice.

When a phone number for public comment is provided, consider using it instead of sending a digital or paper comment. With a cell phone within reach of more and more Americans every day, no matter where they are or what they're doing, making a phone call may be the easiest way to get your opinions recorded. Don't shy away from dialing a comment line for fear of confrontation. If you're calling a hotline set up specifically to receive public comments, the call recipient would be remiss to confront you. They are expecting your call and their job is to record your comments—that's all. With either e-mails or phone calls, remember that it's not only okay to be brief, it's preferable. So don't be daunted by what is really a simple task. Keeping quiet is not an option if you want to see new environmental programs, tougher environmental regulations and stricter enforcement of them.

WHERE TO TAKE ACTION ONLINE

The organizations starting on page 133 are empowering busy people to take action online and make a difference. At the time of publication, the information on these Web sites was accurate. Some of them may have added or discontinued activist tools; some may have changed their URL. Such change is to be expected from the Web. Navigating these sites to find their action alerts is usually quite easy. From their respective home pages, look for and follow links with names like *Action Alerts, Campaigns, Take Action* or *Get Involved.*

Once you've identified some organizations that are working on issues near and dear to you, sign up for their e-mail alerts. This will help you stay informed on pet issues and ensure that opportunities to respond to time-sensitive action alerts won't be missed. It will also save you the time of having to check-in on a Web site to see what's new.

AIR

American Lung Association
◉ ✍ 📧

Public advocate for clean air, as well as the chief source of information and public education on the health hazards of air pollution.
lungaction.org

Clear the Air Campaign
◉ ✍ 📧

Working to improve air quality by reducing emissions from coal-burning power plants.
cleartheair.org

ENERGY AND TRANSPORTATION

Alliance to Save Energy
◉ 📧

Coalition of prominent business, government, environmental and consumer leaders who promote the efficient use of energy worldwide to benefit consumers, the environment, economy and national security.
ase.org

League of American Bicyclists
◉ ✍

Through advocacy and education, working for a bicycle-friendly America.
bikeleague.org

Clean Car Campaign
◉ ✍

Getting the word out to automakers that citizens want vehicles made available that have higher fuel efficiency and lower emissions.
cleancarcampaign.org

Nuclear Information and Resource Service
◉ ✒ 📧

A national information and networking center for citizens and environmental activists concerned about nuclear power, radioactive waste, radiation and sustainable energy issues.
nirs.org

CORPORATE AND GOVERNMENT ACCOUNTABILITY

Corporate Watch

Fights for corporate accountability, human rights and social and environmental justice.
corpwatch.org

Corporate Accountability International

Challenges irresponsible and dangerous corporate actions around the world.
stopcorporateabusenow.org

Co-op America

Works to stop abusive corporate practices and to create healthy, just and sustainable practices through collective economic action and activism.
coopamerica.org

League of Conservation Voters

Devoted to shaping a pro-environment Congress and White House.
lcv.org

Common Cause

Committed to promoting open, honest and accountable government and to giving citizens a voice in the political process.
commoncause.org

Green Scissors

Working to cut wasteful and environmentally harmful spending in government.
greenscissors.org

Government Accountability Project

Promotes government and corporate accountability by advancing occupational free speech, defending whistleblowers and empowering citizen activists.
whistleblower.org

FOOD AND AGRICULTURE

The Campaign to Label Genetically Engineered Food

Working to get legislation passed that will require the labeling of genetically engineered foods in the United States.
thecampaign.org

Center for Food Safety

Challenges harmful food production technologies and promotes sustainable alternatives.
foodsafetynow.org

GRACE Factory Farm Project

Working to eliminate factory farming in favor of more humane, healthful, economically viable and environmentally sound farming

"The probability that we may fail in the struggle ought not to deter us from the support of a cause we believe to be just." **Abraham Lincoln**

practices. Their Guide to Confronting a CAFO helps citizens organize and fight factory farms at the grassroots level.
factoryfarm.org

Genetically Engineered Food Alert

Facilitates the public's support for the mandatory labeling of genetically engineered food.
gefoodalert.org

Keep Antibiotics Working

Working to end the overuse and misuse of antibiotics in animal agriculture that is leading to antibiotic resistance.
keepantibioticsworking.com

Organic Consumers Association

Fights for public policy that will place a global moratorium on genetically engineered foods and crops; stop factory farming and phase out industrial agriculture; and convert U.S. agriculture to at least 30 percent organic.
organicconsumers.org

Pesticide Action Network North America

Works to replace pesticide use with ecologically sound and socially just alternatives.
panna.org

The True Food Network

Working to end the use of genetically engineered ingredients in our foods.
truefoodnetwork.com

VoteHemp.com

Works to create acceptance of and a free market for industrial hemp.
votehemp.com

GENERAL
Action Network

Network of environmental organizations using a common electronic activism system to inform and empower activists.
actionnetwork.org

Center for Environmental Citizenship

Dedicated to educating, training and organizing a diverse, national network of young leaders to protect the environment.
envirocitizen.org

Earth Island Institute

Supports projects that promote the conservation, preservation and restoration of the global environment.
earthisland.org

Environmental Defense

Dedicated to protecting the environmental rights of all people; among these, clean air, clean water, healthy food and a flourishing ecosystem. They are working to create innovative, equitable and cost-effective solutions to the most urgent environmental problems.
edf.org

Friends of the Earth

Dedicated to preserving the health and diversity of the planet for future generations in part by empowering citizens to have an influential voice in decisions affecting their environment.
foe.org

Greenpeace USA

Uses nonviolent, creative confrontation to expose global environmental problems, and to force solutions that are essential to a green and peaceful future.
greenpeaceusa.org

National Environmental Trust

Informs citizens about environmental problems and how they affect our health and quality of life.
environet.policy.net

Natural Resource Defense Council

Uses law, science and the support of more than 1 million members nationwide to protect the planet's wildlife and wild places and to ensure a safe and healthy environment for all living things.
nrdc.org

National Wildlife Federation

Working to protect America's wildlife since 1936.
nwf.org

Public Citizen's Critical Mass Energy and Environment Program

Seeks policies that will further develop clean-energy alternatives, advocates for sustainable agriculture and works to protect water resources.
citizen.org/cmep

The Public Interest Research Groups (PIRG)

Takes action that protects the environment, encourages a fair marketplace for consumers and fosters responsive, democratic government.
pirg.org

"If we do not change our direction, we are likely to end up where we are headed." **Chinese proverb**

Save Our Environment Action Center

Collaborative effort of the nation's most influential environmental advocacy organizations harnessing the power of the Internet to increase public awareness and activism on today's most important issues.
saveourenvironment.org

Union of Concerned Scientists

An alliance of scientists, engineers and citizens disseminating real facts on environmental science to government and the media to effect policy and citizenry for a cleaner, healthier environment and a safer world.
ucsusa.org

The Wilderness Society

Works to protect America's wilderness and to develop a nationwide network of wildlands through public education, scientific analysis and advocacy.
wilderness.org

LAND AND FORESTS
Alliance for the Wild Rockies

Dedicated to protecting and restoring the ecological integrity of the Wild Rockies Bioregion, encompassing the five-state region of Idaho, Montana, Wyoming, eastern Oregon and Washington—and two Canadian provinces, Alberta and British Columbia.
wildrockiesalliance.org

American Lands Alliance

Advocates sound forest and wildlands protection and restoration policy.
americanlands.org

BioGems: A Project of the National Resources Defense Council

Works to save wildlands of exceptional value that are imperiled by logging, mining, oil drilling or other commercial exploitation.
savebiogems.org

Forests.org

Works to end deforestation, preserve old-growth forests, conserve and manage other forests, and commence the age of ecological restoration.
forests.org

Forest Ethics

Works to protect forests by redirecting marketplace activities towards ecologically sound alternatives.
forestethics.org

> "They always say time changes things, but you actually have to change them yourself." **Andy Warhol**

Forests Forever

Protects and enhances the forests and wildlife habitat of California through educational, legislative and electoral activities.
forestsforever.org

Earthworks

Dedicated to protecting communities and the environment from the destructive impacts of mining and mineral development.
earthworksaction.org

Native Forest Council

Exists to preserve and protect all publicly owned natural resources.
forestcouncil.org

Rainforest Action Network

Works to protect tropical rainforests and the human rights of those living in and around them.
ran.org

The Wilderness Society

Using science, advocacy and education, the Wilderness Society is working to protect America's wilderness.
wilderness.org

OCEANS AND CORAL REEFS

Ocean Conservancy

Committed to protecting ocean environments and conserving the global abundance and diversity of marine life.
oceanconservancy.org

Marine Fish Conservation Network

Working to make conservation a top priority of marine fisheries management.
conservefish.org

Oceana

Works to reduce ocean pollution and to prevent the irreversible collapse of fish populations, marine mammals and other sea life.
oceana.org

Reef Relief

Exists to increase public awareness of the importance of living coral reef ecosystems and to protect these ecosystems by encouraging ecotourism and implementing marine protection strategies.
reefrelief.org

ReefKeeper International

Dedicated to the protection of coral reefs and their marine life.
reefkeeper.org

PARKS

Greater Yellowstone Coalition

Works to protect Yellowstone National Park and the land that surrounds it.
greateryellowstone.org

National Parks Conservation Association

Fights to safeguard the scenic beauty, wildlife, and historical and cultural treasures of the largest and most diverse park system in the world.
npca.org

POPULATION

Population Action International

Working to strengthen public awareness and political and financial support worldwide for population programs.
populationaction.org

Population Connection

Working to slow population growth and achieve a sustainable balance between the Earth's people and its resources.
populationconnection.org

The Population Institute

Seeks to reduce excessive population growth to achieve a world population in balance with a healthy global environment and resource base.
populationinstitute.org

RIVERS

American Rivers

Dedicated to protecting and restoring America's river systems and to fostering a river stewardship ethic.
amrivers.org

Trout Unlimited

Works to conserve, protect and restore North America's trout and salmon fisheries and their watersheds.
tu.org

WILDLIFE

Audubon Society

Dedicated to conserving and restoring natural ecosystems, focusing on birds and other wildlife for the benefit of humanity and the earth's biological diversity.
audubon.org

Caribbean Conservation Corporation

Works to protect sea turtles and marine and coastal ecosystems.
cccturtle.org

Center for Biological Diversity

Protecting endangered species and wild places through science, policy, education and environmental law.
biologicaldiversity.org

Defenders of Wildlife

Dedicated to the protection of all native wild animals and plants in their natural communities.
defenders.org

Endangered Species Coalition

Working to ensure that the Endangered Species Act, as well as the species it protects, can be passed on safely into the future.
stopextinction.org

International Fund for Animal Welfare

Works to reduce commercial trade in wild animals, to help animals in crisis and to protect habitat for animals.
ifaw.org

Save Our Wild Salmon

Dedicated to bringing back Northwest salmon and steelhead by restoring damaged salmon habitat, including partially dismantling four dams on the Lower Snake River.
wildsalmon.org

Save the Manatee

Engaged in conservation efforts to save endangered manatees from extinction.
savethemanatee.org

World Wildlife Fund

Leads international efforts to protect endangered species and their habitats.
worldwildlife.org

ZERO WASTE AND RECYCLING

GrassRoots Recycling Network

Advocates policies and practices to achieve zero waste, to end corporate welfare for waste and to create sustainable jobs from discards.
grrn.org

Silicon Valley Toxics Coalition

Addresses the environmental and human health problems caused by the rapid growth of the high-tech electronics industry by advancing environmental sustainability and clean production in the industry.
svtc.org/svtc

MORE INFORMATION

Other environmental organizations that have either not gotten around to integrating e-activism technology into their Web sites or disagree with its use and effectiveness are doing good work. Below are some excellent online directories that categorize environmental organizations by topic.

The Envirolink Network Library of Organizations: *envirolink.org*

WebActive: *webactive.com/page/directory*

Rachel's: *rachel.org/orglist/*

To get in touch with your government officials, you have a choice of several good Web sites:

Capital Advantage's Congress.org: *congress.org*

The U.S. Government's Official Web Portal: *firstgov.com*

U.S. House of Representatives: *house.gov*

U.S. Senate: *senate.gov*

CHAPTER 7:
RESOURCES TO HELP THE EARTH

The Internet has grown into a vast resource that can put us on the fast track to communication, education and enlightenment. And Internet usage is an ever-increasing part of mainstream life: some 72 percent of American adults go online at least once a month.[1]

Just about anything you want to know or find is now, or soon will be, on the Internet. However, the likelihood that what you seek exists somewhere in cyberspace and the feasibility of finding it are two separate things entirely. Finding what you're looking for among over 4 billion pages, give or take a few million, can be a frustrating task. Online searches are often exhausting and incomplete and their results erroneous. For busy people who can't or won't spend the time searching, the Internet just isn't that useful.

If your hopes for utilizing the Internet as an information portal have been dashed one too many times because of its vastness, don't despair. By using the Web sites identified in this chapter, the Internet can be that efficient, helpful resource that, as a busy person, you can use and rely on for quick answers and more information on subjects of both popular and critical importance to successful greener living.

THE IMPORTANCE OF BEING BETTER INFORMED

The environment—complicated, misunderstood and recondite—suffers when the masses fail to understand how to reduce their ecological footprint. Decisions based on a lack of knowledge or misinformation can and do lead to errors in judgment, or simply oversights, with unintentional consequences. And oftentimes people act hastily or negligently when they know better, but do so because solutions elude them precisely when they are needed. Information is invaluable to forming decisions and making choices that can better protect our world, but we can't be experts on everything—and we don't need to be. Taking advantage of what the Internet has to offer, an able and willing individual can access information on just about any subject.

A click of the mouse can now put information before you that previously was only attainable through industrious searches through libraries of one sort or another or by special request. Access to timely and extensive information and viewpoints via the Internet not only leads to a more informed citizenry, but it is also requisite for revolutionizing our thoughts and living habits, since daily choices and habits are an outgrowth of what we know and believe. A pursuit of knowledge that can impart wisdom and reveal solutions is essential to making intelligent, deliberate and purposeful decisions in our lives.

INFORMATION THE BUSY PERSON CAN USE

Granted, the Internet is a vast oasis of information, but it is also a free-for-all—a conglomeration of sites of credible and dubious origin and purpose, the merited and the inappropriate, the intelligent as well as the inane, and the verbose versus the laconic. With so much to sort through, the trick to getting quick, applicable results from the Internet may be to have someone else do the sorting. And on certain matters of environmental importance, this book has done just that.

The only satisfactory end result to using the Web sites selected below, is that busy people can trust and make use of what is provided to become a smarter, more productive and effectual steward of the environment. For a Web site, or specific Web page as the case may be, to be deemed suitable, it had to satisfy the following criteria:

- It covers a subject of either popular or critical importance.
- The content is concise and to the point.
- The presentation and explanation are clear and straightforward.
- The source is credible and reliable.

Not all resources will perfectly meet these criteria in the eyes of the discriminating reader; nonetheless, the resources herein

"If anyone can show me, and prove to me, that I am wrong in thought or deed, I will gladly change. I seek the truth, which never yet hurt anybody. It is only persistence in self-delusion and ignorance which does harm."
Marcus Aurelius

provide excellent information that can prepare you to make better decisions for yourself and the environment.

Some of the Web page addresses, or URLs (URL stands for Uniform Resource Locator), provided below are longer than you may be used to seeing. These longer URLs circumvent the site's home page, taking you instantly deeper into its directories and substantive content. Bypassing a Web site's home page can save the busy person a lot of time, but there can be a down side: due to the dynamic and constantly changing nature of the Web, site administrators sometimes modify URLs faster than any printed index can keep up with them. You have a few options if you type one of the URLs provided below into your Internet browser's window and are served an error message:

1. Revert to the Web site's home page address (the home page address is comprised of all characters preceding the first forward slash), and navigate the site until you find a link to the referenced information.
2. From the Web site's home page, locate the "Contact Us" or "E-mail" link, and send a request for the updated URL and wait for a reply.

> **To link to these Web pages, visit this book's companion Web site at *greenmatters.com* and click on "Helpful Links."**

Of course, other good resources on the following, and other, subjects can be found online. When surfing the Internet, use a search engine that ranks high in terms of delivering accurate results. Google has earned consistently high marks for relevant searches, overall usability and comprehensive results. You can find the latest reviews of Internet search engines at Search Engine Watch (*searchenginewatch.com*) or Search Engine Showdown (*searchengineshowdown.com*). Once you select a search engine, navigate that site for its search tips. Every engine is a little different, and knowing how to use a particular one will refine your search results, increasing what you can achieve online in less time.

BUILDING AND HOME IMPROVEMENT

Whether building a new home or remodeling an existing one, every decision you make has consequences to the environment. In new home construction, your choice for site location, home size, design, and material and product specification will determine your home's impact on the environment now and for years to come. When remodeling, responsible dismantling and disposal are just as important as planning for the addition or renovation. Generally, a home should not exceed what you need and construction and design should include the application of nontoxic, renewable and low-impact materials and technologies to the fullest extent possible.

buildinggreen.com
Informative articles and a comprehensive directory of green building products are available to Web site subscribers, or buy a hard copy of the GreenSpec directory, with over 1,400 product descriptions, environmental characteristics and considerations, and manufacturer contact information.

greenhomebuilding.com
Provides a good introduction to different sustainable building considerations with links to books and an "Expert Advice" Q&A forum.

greenbuilder.com/sourcebook
Information on green building systems and materials including definitions, considerations, market status, implementation issues and guidelines.

oikos.com/products
Search by product type to find manufacturers of sustainable building materials and finishes.

usgbc.org
Locate a builder accredited by the U.S. Green Building Council under their Leadership in Energy and Environmental Design Program (LEED).

salvageweb.com
build.recycle.net
If your city is short on businesses that cater to those wanting to take advantage of architectural salvage and used building materials, try searching one of these online materials exchanges.

rehabadvisor.pathnet.org
Guidelines for conducting an energy-efficient house renovation.

eartheasy.com/live_nontoxic_paints.htm
Find an excellent article on how to choose safer paint coatings.

organicarchitect.com/pdf/countertops.pdf
This article will help the kitchen remodeler sort out the eco-benefits, the eco-impacts and the relative costs of several countertop materials.

CORPORATE ACCOUNTABILITY AND CONSUMER PROTECTION
Corporations' profit-driven interests often overpower consideration for the well-being of natural resources, the environment and public health. With the help of watchdog organizations that specialize in investigating and reporting on criminal or deleterious acts by corporations, you'll know when and why to pull your support of a company.

corpwatch.org
Information on corporate improprieties every consumer should know about.

prwatch.org
Get the facts behind misleading public relations campaigns designed to trick consumers and voters.

responsibleshopper.org
Before you buy, learn more about the companies behind the products. A searchable database allows the user to find reports on over 350 different companies.

eco-labels.org
The Consumers Union's searchable database of eco-labels allows users to review an independent evaluation of several labels used on food, personal hygiene, household cleaners, and wood and paper products.

chemicalindustryarchives.org
The real and present danger of many widely used chemicals has motivated chemical manufacturers to spend a great deal of money to "convince" the public that we have nothing to worry about, but we do, as documents at this Web site attest.

ENERGY

Nationally, our reliance primarily on fossil fuels for electricity has taken a sizeable toll on the environment. The burning of fossil fuels such as coal, gas and oil is the leading man-made cause of ozone depleting CO_2 and the second leading cause of smog-forming nitrogen oxide. And massive hydro-power dams have forever altered the natural flow of rivers and devastated native fish populations by inhibiting their migration. Conserving energy at home and work, and switching to renewable, clean energy sources will help to diminish the need for, and the effects of, dirty and nature-altering sources of power.

www.eere.energy.gov
www.nrel.gov
www.repp.org
These energy information sites provide information on renewable-energy technologies, energy facts and figures, and resources for further learning.

energystar.gov/products
Make energy-efficient choices when buying appliances, electronics, lighting, etc. Energy Star, a project of the U.S. EPA, tests and qualifies energy-efficient products in thirty-eight product categories. Identify Energy Star–rated products and locate stores through their Web site.

homeenergy.org/hewebsite/consumerinfo/ lighting
Convert watts and calculate savings between incandescent and fluorescent bulbs.

hes.lbl.gov
energystar.gov/index.cfm?c=home_improve-ment.hm_improvement_index_tools
Do-it-yourself energy audit tools. Enter details about your home and learn of upgrades that can save energy and money.

doityourself.com/doors/more.htm
Improve the energy efficiency of existing windows or choose replacement windows for your climate with the help of this easy-to-understand guide.

dsireusa.org
The Database of State (and Federal) Incentives for Renewable Energy (DSIRE) is a source of information on state, local, utility and selected federal incentives that promote renewable energy.

green-e.org
Learn how to support renewable energy through renewable energy brokers or Tradable Renewable Energy Certificates.

woodheat.org
Whether burning wood for heat or ambience, do it efficiently and follow the suggestions and guidelines provided by the Wood Heat Organization.

GARDENING AND LAWN CARE

Environmentally friendly land management relies, in part, on native landscaping, efficient watering, and nonchemical treatments for fertilizing and controlling unwanted pests. Planning landscapes and gardens that are low-maintenance and use plants native to the area will reduce the water they require beyond that provided by average, regional precipitation. Native landscapes will also provide shelter and nutrients for animals and insects, promoting a balanced and healthy ecosystem around your house. When fertilization or pest management is called for, applying organic treatments will assist the survival of all living things in the air, soil and water around your home.

wildflower2.org
plantnative.org
Provides assistance in the cultivation and preservation of native flora with directories of suppliers, helpful organizations and specific plant information.

nwf.org/backyardwildlifehabitat
The National Wildlife Federation will help you create a wildlife habitat in your backyard through their Backyard Wildlife Habitat Program.

richsoil.com/lawn
Organic lawn-care steps and principles anyone can understand and follow.

> "Men occasionally stumble over the truth, but most of them pick themselves up and hurry off as if nothing ever happened."
> **Sir Winston Churchill**

icangarden.com/document.cfm?task=viewdetail&itemid=734
"Xeriscaping," by Julie Ferraro, covers the basics of water-wise landscaping. Related links to more articles and books to help you get started are conveniently located in the right-margin table of contents.

organicgardening.com/steps
Organic gardening basics are covered with articles and related links on building healthy soil, controlling weeds without chemicals, and growing specific vegetables and flowers organically.

gardensablaze.com/companions.htm
Learn which plants, planted side by side in your garden, can provide natural pest management and improve yields.

ipm.ucdavis.edu/PMG/crops-agriculture.html
This online pest identification and management guide from The University of California Integrated Pest Management Program is superb if used properly. It's helpful for identifying diseases and pests through descriptions and pictures, and in many cases recommends Organically Acceptable Methods of management.

beyondpesticides.org
Information on specific pesticides, "least toxic" alternatives for controlling yard and garden pests, a directory of service providers and lots more information to help you control pesticide use in your community.

batcon.org
Learn where to buy or how to build a Bat Conservation International–approved bat house for the purpose of natural and very effective pest control.

digitalseed.com/composter
Information on home composting that demonstrates how easy it can be.

recycleworks.org/compost/compingr.html
A list of what can and should not be added to the compost pile.

greyhoundmanor.com/pat/compost/pooppat.html
One of the few online resources for how to compost dog waste.

southface.org
For a guide to simple rainwater collection for landscaping, click on "Resources & Services" from the home page, then "Fact Sheets," and then scroll down until you find the link to "Rainwater Recovery."

**"The end of the human race will be that it will eventually die of civilization."
Ralph Waldo Emerson**

GLOBAL WARMING

The rapid climate change, by historical measures, which the earth has experienced in the last 120 years, is primarily due to human activities like burning fossil fuels. Escalating concentrations of greenhouse gases resulting from the combustion of fossil fuels has the effect of trapping heat in the earth's atmosphere. As the earth warms out of step with its natural cycle, glaciers are melting, arctic ice is thinning, ocean levels are rising and coral reefs are dying from overheated waters.

*www.ncdc.noaa.gov/oa/climate/
globalwarming.html*
A scientific yet understandable explanation of global warming.

climate.org
Overview of critical topics related to global warming with links to more resources on each topic.

GREEN CLEANING

During their use, cleaning products can be harmful by way of contact, inhalation or ingestion. And most of the cleaners and solvents used in and outside the home will end up in the environment via storm drains or sewers. If dangerous chemicals are present, vegetation, wildlife and water quality can be affected. Transitioning to green cleaning can be as easy as opening your pantry. Baking soda, vinegar, salt,

lemon juice and olive oil are just some of the ingredients that can be combined to safely and effectively clean your home from top to bottom.

*epa.gov/grtlakes/seahome/housewaste/house/
products.htm*
A glossary of common household products, their hazardous constituents and risks of exposure.

es.epa.gov/techinfo/facts/safe-fs.html
Fast facts on household cleaners, a list of toxic ingredients to avoid, alternatives to commercial products you can whip up yourself and resources for more information.

cnt.org/wetcleaning/final-report/learned
Find out more about professional wet cleaning—a safer alternative to dry cleaning.

nybg.org/plants/factsheets/cleanair.html
Houseplants that can improve indoor air quality.

LIVABLE COMMUNITIES

Sprawl has increased automobile dependence, seen vast tracts of open space and farmland paved over, isolated suburbanites from vibrant community centers, and brought industrial zones and residential communities closer to each other. The adverse impacts to wildlife, air, water and our quality of life has incited several organizations to design and promote anti-sprawl packages to help citizens organize and combat thoughtless development.

As for the not-so-visible assaults on our communities, Internet databases are helping citizens identify polluters by zip code. Once polluters have been identified, you can share your findings and concerns with community leaders and local or state environmental advocacy groups to induce corrective action.

empowermentinstitute.net/files/LNP.html
The Livable Neighborhood Program promotes initiatives designed to work at the neighborhood level to improve the overall livability of communities.

sierraclub.org/sprawl
The Sierra Club identifies both the problems and solutions of sprawl and directs the reader to resources for further reading in their comprehensive online guide to stopping sprawl.

ceds.org
Download Community & Environmental Defense Services' free publication, "Preserving Neighborhoods & the Environment from Unsustainable Land Development Projects: A Citizen's Guide to Forming a Winning Strategy"—a guide to 150 actions found to be most effective in identifying and preventing the impacts of development projects.

bikewalk.org
This site can help you create neighborhoods and communities where people walk and bicycle.

lta.org/conserve/index.html
nature.org/joinanddonate/giftandlegacy
Protect your undeveloped land from the threat of development. Land Trust Alliance and The Nature Conservancy explain options that are open to landowners who want their land protected now or for the future.

darksky.org
Learn how to fight light pollution in your community.

scorecard.org
rtk.net
How insulated is your community from polluters? Retrieve available information on local pollution and who's responsible from these online databases.

communitygreens.org
pps.org
Resources, case studies, and publications to help citizens create or preserve parks and public spaces that build and nurture communities.

cohousing.org
Find out more about eco/community living options that can conserve land and foster community.

MEDIA

The increasingly corporate-controlled media is arguably limiting the viewpoints we have access to. In broadcast news in particular, there is evidence of misdirected journalistic priorities, obvious political biases, a compulsion to sensationalize events and spinning news stories to influence public opinion. A certain amount of frustration and skepticism on the part of viewers is justified, but don't stew or settle—seek out the truth and find alternatives to mainstream news broadcasts and publications.

fair.org

Fairness and Accuracy in Reporting, by exposing well-documented examples of media bias and censorship, is making it a little easier for news watchers to know who to trust for honest and diverse reporting. Access the latest edition of their weekly radio program CounterSpin, for news that mainstream media isn't reporting.

prwatch.org/spin

The Center for Media and Democracy's daily bulletin entitled Spin of the Day reports on spin and propaganda in the media from the previous news day.

altpress.org
alternet.org
mediachannel.org
npr.org

Use these resources for better access to independent and alternative journalism.

OFFICE/BUSINESS

Waste management and energy use are increasing concerns for businesses—and an opportunity to lower operating costs and increase profits. Several state and federal programs are working to assist businesses in implementing waste reduction, recycling and energy-wise programs to improve the bottom line while providing relief to the environment.

It's not just what's going on inside office buildings that is cause for increased business participation in solutions that work. Commuting trends have increased transportation-based pollution: the number of people driving to work in a private car has steadily increased since 1985, while the percentage of workers carpooling has declined and transit's share of commuters has changed little. Compounding the effects of increased vehicle use is the increase in distance traveled due to the migration of the American family away from city and business centers.[2] Solutions for commuters can and should encompass employer assistance since several studies show that implementing work options that reduce commuting, such as compressed work weeks and telecommuting, increase employee productivity and retention.[3]

naturalstep.org

Helps visionary companies achieve sustainability and profitability through cost savings and product and service innovation.

"Human history becomes more and more a race between education and catastrophe." **H. G. Wells**

greenbiz.com
Provides businesses with access to tools and information that can facilitate their transition to more sustainable business practices.

environmentaldefense.org/alliance/officetips. html
A handy guide for office personnel on greening the office.

epa.gov/epaoswer/non-hw/reduce/wstewise
The EPA's WasteWise program helps interested businesses develop, implement and measure waste-reduction activities to eliminate costly municipal solid waste, benefiting the bottom line and the environment.

epa.gov/greenpower/join
Join the EPA's Green Power Partnership and commit to the purchase of green power. Available assistance, tool kits and resources help partners purchase green power and promote their involvement in the program.

safeclimate.net/business/index.php
epa.gov/climateleaders
Information and tools to help businesses of any size begin to manage their greenhouse gas emissions, demonstrate leadership and make a meaningful impact on the climate.

ofee.gov/recycled/cal-index.htm
This easy-to-use paper calculator allows you to compare the environmental impacts of paper with different post-consumer recycled content.

rethinkpaper.org
Determine which tree-free or recycled-content paper best fits your needs with the interactive "Paper Selector."

svtc.org/cleancc/index.html
Silicon Valley Toxics Coalition's annual scorecard of the most environmentally responsible computer companies.

techrecycle.com
interconrecycling.com
recyclingsupersite.com
Business solutions for recycling obsolete computers and eliminating storage and disposal liabilities. See also, *Reduce, Reuse and Recycle* on page 154.

commuterchoice.gov
Enroll your business in the Commuter Choice program and get help adopting solutions that reduce commuter driving.

sustainablebusiness.com/jobs
Whether hiring or looking to be hired, this is one of the most current and comprehensive databases of job openings at sustainable businesses or within the environmental field. If you want to post a résumé, try *greenbiz.com/jobs.*

POPULATION AND THE ENVIRONMENT

By many accounts, the explosive population growth over the past forty years has been the largest contributing factor to environmental degradation. Increased demand for housing, food, water, fuel and nonessential consumables is stressing the earth beyond its capacity to regenerate. If you think the population problem and solution resides with the developing countries that out populate the United States by 3 to 1, think again. The average American consumes over twenty-five times more resources than the average person from a developing country.[4] The World Wildlife Fund's annual Living Planet Report estimates that the human population and resource consumption has surpassed the earth's carrying capacity. If current tendencies in reproduction and consumption do not change, we will experience the complete collapse of critical ecological assets this century.[5]

populationaction.org/issues
worldpopulationbalance.org/pop
Fact sheets and answers to questions about population and natural resources.

plannedparenthood.org/health
Voluntary family-planning resources.

myfootprint.org
Test your ecological footprint.

REDUCE, REUSE AND RECYCLE

Most people associate recycling with admirable environmental stewardship. However, recycling is the third step in a three-step process. Effective waste reduction and resource protection relies on first reducing the amount we consume; second, reusing that which still has a useful life; and third, recycling when something is beyond repair or reuse.

isharestuff.org
This site helps you share specific belongings, e.g., high-cost or seldom-used things, with family and friends. Whether it's your pickup truck or a hot-glue gun, useful things you own, and want your friends to know you'll lend, can be posted here and they'll be notified. Before you know it, people you'll lend to will start their own accounts and post things you can borrow from them.

freecycle.org
craigslist.org
The surest and fastest way to find a second home for acceptable quality items you no longer have a use for is to give them away for free. Post items, or look for things yourself, at one of these Web sites organized by city.

mothering.com/articles/new_baby/diapers/
  joy-of-cloth.html
thediaperhyena.com
Find almost everything you ever wanted or needed to know about cloth diapering.

"If future generations are to remember us with gratitude rather than contempt, we must leave them something more than the miracles of technology. We must leave them a glimpse of the world as it was in the beginning, not just after we got through with it." **Lyndon B. Johnson**

fleamarketguide.com
collectors.org/FM
For used merchandise, get acquainted with flea markets, swap meets and antiques fairs in your region.

obviously.com/recycle
Obvious Implementation Corporation's online recycling guide is full of valuable information on basic recycling, recycling obscure materials and reducing unwanted junk mail.

earth911.org
Provide your zip code upon entering the Web site to locate municipal recycling centers or to find out where to recycle specific items. Don't assume something can't be recycled or donated for reuse until you've checked here first.

wirelessfoundation.org/DonateaPhone
collectivegood.com
wirelessrecycling.com
Donate used wireless phones. They will either be refurbished for a charity in need or recycled in an environmentally sound manner.

greendisk.com
ecodisk.com
Recycling solutions for your personal or business media products and more.

techsoup.org/recycle/10tips.cfm
If you're going to donate an old computer, do it right; follow Compumentor's "Ten Tips for Donating a Computer."

epa.gov/epaoswer/osw/conserve/plugin
The EPA, through its Plug-In To eCycling campaign, is making it easier to recycle electronics by indexing businesses that take back used and obsolete electronics.

ciwmb.ca.gov/RCP
The Recycled Content Product Directory, a project of California's Integrated Waste Management Board is a searchable database of all kinds of recycled products. You can even specify a minimum recycled content for your search results.

SAFE FOOD AND SUSTAINABLE AGRICULTURE

To achieve sustainable agriculture and protect the food supply, our agricultural practices must succeed in protecting area, biodiversity, topsoil, water supply and livestock health. Consumer buying trends will determine what is produced and will drive the policy that regulates agriculture. Therefore, your informed purchases are needed to send the appropriate and intended message to food growers and producers and to the regulatory agencies charged with protecting consumer and agricultural interests alike.

theorganicreport.org
Organic news and articles including "Questions and Answers about Organic" and "Buying Organic: Considering the Real Costs."

factoryfarm.org
GRACE's Family Farm Project defines the factory farm and provides current news and information about factory farm issues by topic (e.g., dairy, poultry, fish, etc.) and region.

gene-watch.org/programs/food/foodFAQ. html
foei.org/gmo/faq.html
Frequently asked questions on GMOs are answered by the Council for Responsible Genetics and Friends of the Earth International.

foe.org/safefood/companylist.html
In the absence of a labeling system for GE foods, Friends of the Earth has compiled a list to help consumers identify companies known to use GE ingredients.

truefoodnow.org/shoppersguide
The True Food Shopping Guide identifies GE-free brands in several categories.

ucsusa.org/food_and_environment/biotech-nology/page.cfm?pageID=337
The Union of Concerned Scientists' guide to GE crops allowed in the U.S. food supply.

renewableenergyworks.com/sustainability/ meatless.html
The environmental consequences of eating meat are summarized in "Eating Green: A Re-examination of Diet in Light of Environmental Concerns," by Walter Simpson. Simpson's article touches on nearly all the major issues including inefficient land use, water scarcity and pollution, loss of biodiversity, depletion of fossil fuels, global warming, deforestation, and native species decline.

veg.ca/living/veg-position-paper.html
Learn more about a vegetarian diet, which can be healthful, nutritionally adequate, and provide health benefits in the prevention and treatment of certain diseases.

localharvest.org
Search for farmers' markets, family farms, food co-ops and restaurants selling locally produced, organic food.

csacenter.org
Community Supported Agriculture (CSA) connects local farms with local consumers, encourages land stewardship, develops a regional food supply and strong local economy, and promotes the economic viability of small, family farms. This site enables visitors to locate CSA farms by state or get help forming a CSA network.

eatwellguide.org
Enter your zip code to find where you can

buy sustainably raised meat, poultry, dairy and eggs near your home.

foodnews.org
A report card of the best and worst produce choices relative to pesticide contamination.

mbayaq.org/cr/seafoodwatch.asp
Monterey Bay Aquarium's Seafood Watch program educates shoppers on the least to most sustainable seafood choices. From their Web site, download a free wallet-size chart to refer to when buying seafood.

farmtoschool.org
Transform your child's school lunch program into one that supports local farmers, sustainability and healthy food choices.

thehia.org/hempfacts.htm
abouthemp.com
If you haven't heard about industrial hemp yet, it's time you knew of its history, vast applications and superior qualities. Refer to chapter 5 to locate hemp products and support the hemp industry.

TRANSPORTATION

It's been said that driving a car is the single most polluting thing the average person does in a day. Biking, walking, ride sharing, consolidating trips and taking public transportation when feasible are alternatives that pay big dividends to the environment. Short of leaving the car at home, adopting better driving habits and driving a low-emissions vehicle can help reduce the impacts from driving.

Automobiles aren't the only mode of transportation relying on expanded infrastructure, emitting greenhouse gases, and consuming scarce and finite petroleum supplies, but because they are the main source of transportation for most Americans, what we drive, how we drive and how often we drive stands to make the biggest reduction in transportation-related environmental impacts.

bts.gov/publications/national_transportation_statistics/
Statistics reveal a conspicuous addiction to cars and very real impacts. If you like numbers, this site has lots: tables on motor vehicle fuel consumption and travel, annual wasted fuel due to congestion, principle means of transportation to work, public road and street mileage, air pollution trends, and over 200 others.

greenercars.com/bestof
The best and worst cars for the environment.

epa.gov/greenvehicles
Look up cars and trucks by vehicle class or a specific model to find scores on air pollution, fuel economy and greenhouse gas emissions.

> "The mystery of a government is not how Washington works, but how to make it stop." **P. J. O'Rourke**

fueleconomy.gov
Find and compare cars side by side on fuel economy, greenhouse gas emissions and air pollution. This site also explains how you can earn a federal income tax deduction if purchasing a "clean-fuel" vehicle before the end of 2006.

suv.org/introductory.html
This site is designed solely to educate consumers on the impacts and dangers of driving an SUV.

fuelcells.org
Vehicles that run on fuel cells are in development and will be available soon. Learn more about the technology and the benefits to the environment.

biodieselamerica.org
biodiesel.org
Information on renewable biodiesel for diesel engines.

runmuki.com/commute
Cycling activist Paul Dorn offers prospective bike commuters tips to make the transition from car to bike easy, safe and fun.

erideshare.com
vanpool.com
Get help connecting with other commuters going your way.

metrocommuterservices.org/costcal.asp
Calculate the cost of driving a car and add it to the many environmental reasons to drive less.

flexcar.com
Joining a car-sharing service can be much cheaper, and lower impact, than owning a vehicle if you rarely need to drive.

TRAVEL AND RECREATION
Travel and tourism is the world's largest industry, and according to the World Tourism Organization, more and more tourists are visiting sensitive natural places. Travelers and recreationists need to be acutely aware of the powerful impact they have on the natural environment. Whether traveling for business or pleasure, plan ahead so you can minimize the potential negative effects from travel.

ecotour.org
Find travel opportunities that benefit local communities and preserve the environment.

greenhotels.com/members.htm
Identify hotels that are committed to reducing waste, conserving resources and reducing or eliminating the use of chemicals.

triplee.com/environment/carbon_offsets.htm
Offset the greenhouse gas emissions produced from your air travel by joining

Better World Club and booking flights through their Travel Cool Program.

oceanconservancy.org/site/DocServer/ fscruiseships.pdf?docID=102
The impacts of cruise ships on the marine environment.

skiareacitizens.com
This environmental scorecard of ski areas grades over seventy western resorts on their environmental policies and practices. For comparison, the National Ski Area Association maintains a database of specific preservation and conservation programs being implemented by ski areas at **nsaa.org/nsaa/environment/the_greenroom**.

lnt.org
When visiting the outdoors, follow the Principles of Leave No Trace to minimize your impact on the natural environment you're passing through.

nrdc.org/water/oceans/ttw/titinx.asp
Natural Resources Defense Council's annual report of water quality at vacation beaches.

VOTING AND POLITICS
Americans have voiced their concern and support for the environment in national polls, yet the recent congressional record is increasingly in favor of loosening public land-use restrictions and environmental regulations. Reversing this trend will require getting better at evaluating candidates running for public office with the help of trustworthy resources, and keeping the pressure on delegates to act in the interest of their constituents while shunning the influences of large donations.

firstgov.org
This is the U.S. government's official information portal. Link to any agency's Web site; find contact information for elected officials at the local, state and federal level; and look up and comment on federal regulations.

lcv.org/scorecard
The League of Conservation Voters' National Environmental Scorecard provides factual information about the environmental voting records of U.S. Representatives and Senators.

vote-smart.org
Project Vote Smart's Web site is comprised of thoroughly-researched data covering candidates and elected officials. This data includes factual information about their voting records, campaign finances, position statements and backgrounds. Project Vote Smart's National Political Awareness Test (NPAT) is a voluntary, comprehensive questionnaire that allows candidates to reveal their issue inclinations to voters. It is a remarkable tool for voters to learn candidates' issue positions and willingness to provide information to the public.

factcheck.org
This organization reveals factual inaccuracies in the statements of politicians, pundits and spokespeople so voters won't be so easily deceived.

citizen.org/litigation/free_info
Public Citizen assists individuals and organizations in accessing information held by government agencies.

gp.org
lp.org
natural-law.org
reformparty.org
constitutionparty.com
Traditional and entrenched thinking from the predominating political parties may not hold the best solutions for today and tomorrow. The advancement of alternative views comes from many sources. Read what other parties are saying about the environment, government spending, taxes, etc. For a complete list of all political parties, visit **politics1.com/parties.htm.**

opensecrets.org
An educational resource on the problem of money in politics.

congress.org/congressorg/megavote
Track your Senators' and Representative's votes by e-mail with MegaVote.

greensheets.com
Analysis of environment, energy and natural resource issues coming before the U.S. Congress.

regulations.gov
Look up federal documents published in the Federal Register open for public comment.

WATER
Population growth has increased water demand for irrigation, domestic use and industry. In heavy-use regions, withdrawals from surface water supplies and groundwater reserves are so high that supplies are being depleted faster than they can be replenished. Serious water shortages in some regions have led to bitter fights over water rights with devastating outcomes for aquatic ecosystems.

On the side of water quality, agricultural and urban runoff, chemical dumping by industries, and careless use and disposal of household hazardous products all contribute to poor water quality in the United States. Much of our water is too dirty for basic uses such as swimming and fishing, and native species are disappearing from our rivers, lakes and coastal waters.

h2ouse.org
Take a virtual tour of a typical home and learn how to reduce water use at home.

epa.gov/owow/nps/whatis.html
Polluted runoff is the leading cause of water quality impairment. From this page on the EPA's Web site, you can learn about key sources of non-point source pollution and what you can do at home and in your community to protect water quality.

epa.gov/epaoswer/non-hw/muncpl/hhw.htm
A list of common household hazardous waste (HHW) products that should always be disposed of at a HHW treatment center.

waterwest.org
Whether you live in the West, consume its agricultural products or just pay federal taxes, every American should be cognizant of what's happening with water in the West.

NOTES

GREEN LIVING MYTHS

1. Steve Hoffman, "Got Organic? Natural Products Expo West Displays Growing Demand for All Things Natural," GreenMoney Journal (Summer 2004).

MAKING A DIFFERENCE

1. Robert B. Jackson and others, "Water in a Changing World," *Issues in Ecology*, no. 9 (Spring 2001): 14.

2. Derek Reiber, "Perfecting Biodegradable Plastics," GreenTide, Tidepool.org (July 2002).

3. Karen Pickett, "Why We Won't Recycle Plastics," *Earth Island Journal 11*, no. 4 (Fall 1996), earthisland.org archives.

4. Rhode Island Resource Recovery Corporation, "Plastic Bags Can Blow You Away!" (brochure).

5. U.S. Environmental Protection Agency, "10 Fast Facts on Recycling," www.epa.gov (accessed September 2005).

6. Reusablebags.com, "Fast Facts," www.reusablebags.com (accessed September 2005).

7. U.S. Environmental Protection Agency, "How We Use Water in These United States," 4.

8. American Water Works Association, www.awwa.org (accessed January 2003).

9. U.S. Department of Transportation, Bureau of Transportation Statistics, "National Transportation Statistics 2004," Tables 1–11 and 1–32.

10. U.S. Department of Energy, Energy Information Administration, "Emissions of Greenhouse Gases in the United States 2003," Chapter 2: Carbon Dioxide Emissions (December 2004): 19–20.

11. U.S. Department of Energy, Energy Information Administration, Petroleum Products Information Sheet, Tables 1.3 and 2.5 (March 2003).

12. Based on 12,000 annual vehicle miles traveled (VMT) and average gas mileage of twenty-four miles per gallon (mpg).

13. American Meat Institute, "Overview of U.S. Meat and Poultry Production and Consumption" (2003): 2.

14. John Robins, *The Food Revolution,* Conari Press (July 11, 2001).

15. The National Public Lands Grazing Campaign, "Troubles with Livestock Grazing," 1, www.publiclandsranching.org (accessed September 2005).

16. United States Senate Committee on Agriculture, Nutrition & Forestry, "Environmental Risks of Livestock & Poultry Production" (1998).

17. U.S. Environmental Protection Agency, 2000 National Water Quality Survey, Sources of Impairment, www.epa.gov.

18. Bureau of Labor Statistics, "Consumer Expenditures in 2003," Report 986, Table A.

19. Temperate Forest Foundation, "Pulp and Paper," *Eco-Link* 8, no. 2: 3.

20. Resource Conservation Alliance, "Using Less Wood Fact Sheet: Focus on Paper Consumption," www.woodconsumption.org (accessed May 2005).

21. Abromovitz & Mattoon, "Paper Cuts: Recovering the Paper Landscape," Worldwatch Institute (1999).

22. Institute of Scrap Recycling Industries, "Recycling Paper" (pamphlet).

23. U.S. Department of Energy, Energy Information Administration, "Emissions of Greenhouse Gases in the United States 2003," Table 6.

24. U.S. Environmental Protection Agency, "Fast Facts: Energy Efficient Lighting," www.epa.gov (accessed May 2005).

25. Based on 2003 EPA mileage estimates; actual fuel efficiency may vary.

26. U.S Department of Energy, Office of Energy Efficiency and Renewable Energy, "Technology Snapshot—Featuring the Toyota Prius," www.fueleconomy.gov (accessed May 2005).

27. Population-Environment Balance, "U.S. Population Growth—Food, Land, Energy, Water, and the U.S. Economy (Fact Sheet)," www.balance.org (accessed September 2005).

ECO-TIPS FOR LIVING GREENER

1. Daily water savings based on saving two quarts per wash, four times a day: $(293,655,404 \times .02) \times (2 \times 4 \div 4) = 11,746,216$ gallons. Daily energy savings based on reducing cooking time by one-third using a 15,000 BTU gas cooktop for 40 minutes: $(293,655,404 \times .01) \times (15,000 \div 3) = 14,682,770,200$ BTUs.

2. U.S. Environmental Protection Agency, Municipal Solid Waste Commodities Fact Sheet: Plastics 2003, www.epa.gov.

BUYING GREEN

1. U.S. Environmental Protection Agency, Office of Pollution Prevention and Toxics, Chemical Hazard Data Availability Study, www.epa.gov (April 2004).

2. Brad Duplisea, "The Real Dope on Beef Hormones," Canadian Health Coalition, www.healthcoalition.ca (accessed September 2005).

GETTING INVOLVED

1. The USFS's decision was immediately challenged by civil liberties, environmental and business groups alike, and the decision is expected to be overturned.

RESOURCES TO HELP THE EARTH

1. Ipsos-Insight Marketing Research, *The Face of the Web 2004*.

2. U.S. Census Bureau, American Housing Survey for the United States, 1985 and 2003 journey to work statistics.

3. Business for Social Responsibility, Issue Brief on Work-Life, bsr.org (accessed May 2005).

4. World Population Balance, www.world-populationbalance.org (accessed May 2005).

5. World Wildlife Fund International, *Living Planet Report 2004*.

INDEX